Bramha vidya
vol-2

K V Krishnan

BlueRose ONE.com DIY
Stories Matter
NewDelhi • London

BLUEROSE PUBLISHERS
India | U.K.

For permissions requests or inquiries regarding this publication,
please contact:

BLUEROSE PUBLISHERS
www.BlueRoseONE.com
info@bluerosepublishers.com
+91 8882 898 898
+4407342408967

ISBN: 978-93-5819-180-6

First Edition: August 2023

Dedicated to

Acharyas and Lord LakshmiNrisimha

Foreword

Dr. T.K. Parthasarathy, Prof Madras University

Swami Alavandar's Stotra Rathnam , in fact ,is the first Stotra literature on Perumal in Sanskrit (The earlier ones in Sanskrit were all just depicting his qualities-same is the case of Chatusloki on Piratti) and it is but a fitting tribute to the author to include

Contents

1. Prayer

ज्ञानानन्दमयं देवं निर्मल स्फकाकृतिम्।
आधारं सर्व विद्यानां **हयग्रीवम्** उपास्महे॥

अज्ञानतिमिरान्धस्य ज्ञानाञ्जनशलाकया।
चक्षुरुन्मीलितं येन तस्मै श्रीगुरवे नमः॥

गुरुर्ब्रह्मा गुरुर्विष्णुःगुरुर् देवोमहेश्वरः।
गुरुर् साक्षात् परब्रह्म तरमै **श्रीगुरवे** नमः॥

यो नित्यम् अच्युतपदाम्बुजयुग्मरुक्म-
व्यामोहतस्तदितराणि तृणाय मेने ।
अस्मद् गुरोर्भगवतोऽस्य दयैकसिन्धोः
रामानुजस्य चरणौ शरणं प्रपद्ये ॥

श्रीमान् वेङ्कटनाथार्यः कवितार्किककेसरी ।
वेदान्ताचार्यवर्यो मे सन्निधत्तां सदा हृदि ॥

2. Introduction

BramhaVidya - the knowledge of Truth, that results in Self-realization followed by realisation of Bramha m within us, whereby one remains untouched by any situation in life. Bramha m is the neuter gender of the root word-form **"brih"** that means big. As the word big has not been further qualified to reveal its dimension, we must understand that Bramha m, the word means that which is free from all forms of limitation.

ब्रह्म **and Vidya.** ब्रह्म comes from root word ब्ह् means biggest and nothing equal or superior to the same. विद्या, comes from विद्- to know. As the word **big** has not been further qualified to reveal its dimension, we must understand that Bramha m, the word means that which is free from all forms of limitation. Different methods of approaching the Absolute or real truth, the Bramha m, are known as Vidyas or UpAsanAs.

Following pages discusses these various Vidyas (thirty- two as stated in VedA) by means of which the **Jiva or the individual soul attains Bramha n or the Supreme Soul (Liberation from Cycle of Birth and death).** The focus in this article will discuss philosophy as enumerated by Sri. Bhagavat RamAnujar (VishishtAdvaita philosophy). Other major philosophy enumerated by Adi Sankara, the Advaitam concept is also discussed, with the help of Internet sources and Books published by various scholars, Kalakshepams from Specialist Vidwans as given in Bibliography.

The secret of Bramha vidyā is to reveal the real nature of the Ātmā, that is all-pervading, that is like ghee in the milk, that is the source of <u>Atmavidyā</u> and <u>Tapas</u> and to show that everything is in essence one. This is the English translation of the Bramha Upanishad (belonging to the Krishna-Yajurveda).

The purpose of our birth is " To get rid of the cycle of birth and death.(Liberation) This is the essence of yoga, veda and all shastras. But how can one do this while in SamsArA?Should one not carry out routine work?Yes do them the Karmayoga way and follow Nysa vidya which recommends the easiest way to attain Liberation is COMPLETE SURRENDER

3. Bramham as stated In Purusha Suktam

वेदाहमेतं पुरुषं महान्तमादित्यवर्णं तमसःपरस्तात् ।

तमेवविदित्वाति मृत्युमेति नान्यपन्थाविद्यतेयनाय ॥(श्वेताश्वतरोपनिषद्-**8**)

vēdāhamētaṁ puruṣaṁ mahāntamādityavarṇaṁ tamasaḥparastāt |
tamēvaviditvādi mṛtyumēti nānyaḥ panthā vidyatēyanāya||
(Swetasvataropanishad-8)

<u>Meaning of the above mantra:</u>
God is the supreme reality who shines effulgent like the Sun beyond all darkness and exists everywhere. We should know His numerous attributes, and try to experience His presence within us and outside. One passes beyond death only on realizing Him (God-the supreme reality). There is no other way of escape from the cycle of births and deaths.

Escape from the cycle of births and deaths is possible only through **Yogic** discipline, complete faith, affection, in Bramha m and feeling His presence in countless manifestations. (As Lord Krishna advises in Gita- to understand His Avatara Rahasya). A very good **Subhashitani**, about Vidya is given below. Virtually Vidya could give everything including appreciation and pooja by kings. Even if wealth is not with someone if Vidya is there, that is sufficient and those who do not have vidya are equal to पशुः i.e., animal. Vidya is equated to Supreme devata, which is what is **Bramha-Vidya.**

विद्या नाम नरस्य रूपमधिकं प्रच्छन्नगुप्तं धनम्

विद्या भोगकरी यशः सुखकरी विद्या गुरूणां गुरुः ।

विद्या बन्धुजनो विधेषगमने **विद्या परा देवता**

विद्या राजसु पूज्यते न तु धनं विद्याविहीनः पशुः॥

vidyā nāma narasya rūpamadhikaṁ pracchatraguptaṁ dhanaṁ
vidyā bhōgakarī yaśaḥ bukhārī vidyā gurūṇāṁ guruḥ |

Another **Subhashitani** for **VidyA:**

नास्ति विद्या समं सक्षु नास्ति विद्या समं तपः |

नास्ति राग समं दुःखम् नास्ति त्याग समं सुखम् ||

There is no such sight such as knowledge. **(विद्या)** i.e., **by knowledge one can see what cannot be seen by naked eye. Knowledge gives the vision to see beyond some obvious things. That is how by learning Bramha VidyA through a Guru one can see Bramha m. (Maitreyi-VidyA-Refer page no 15/40-Sr No 27)**

There is no Tapha (Hard work let us say) such as Truth. One has to do lot of hard work to be on the side of Truth.

There is no Sorrow such as the desire. There is no happiness such as sacrifice. Who else would be happier and more satisfied, than our own Mother? (nAsti tyAga samam sukham)

4. Contents of the Bramha Upaniṣad

Bramha Upanishad Chapter 5

The temple of human body

In the heart are all gods,
In it the vital breaths also,
In the heart is life and light,
And the threefold thread of the world.

Prāṇa soars to heights when awake and retires during deep sleep states the text, just like the falcon soars in the skies and returns to its nest in the night.

<u>Śaunaka</u> Mahāśala questioned the holy Sage <u>Pippalāda</u> thus: "In this beautiful <u>Bramha pura</u> of body, the fit residence of divine beings, how are (the deities of) Vak, etc., located? How do they function? To whom belongs this power? He to whom this power belongs, what is He?"

Pippalāda then having deeply considered, imparted to him the <u>Bramha vidyā</u> (divine wisdom), that most excellent of all things. "It is <u>Prāṇa</u> (i.e.,) Ātmā. It is Ātmā that exercises this power. It is the life of all <u>Devas.</u> It is their death and (their) life. Bramha n that shines pure, resplendent, and all-pervading, in this divine Bramha pura (of body), rules (all). The Jīva (identifying himself with) the Indriyas, rules them like a spider. The spider throws out from a single thread out of his body a whole web, and draws it into himself by that same thread; so Prāṇa, whenever it goes, draws after it the objects of its creation (Vāk, etc.). During Suṣupti, (the Prāṇa) goes to its seat (Bramha n) through the Nādis . Just as a child obtains happiness without desiring for it (in play), so also Devadatta obtains happiness in Suṣupti. He certainly knows, (being) Param-Jyotis, and the person desiring Jyotis, enjoys bliss in the contemplation of Jyotis. Then he comes back to the dream-plane by the same way, like a caterpillar. It remaining on a blade of grass, first puts forward its foot on another blade in front, conveys its body to it, and having got a firm hold of it, then only leaves the former and not before. So, this is the Jāgrata state. As this (Devadatta) bears at the same time eight skulls, so this Jāgrata, the source of Devas and Vedas, clings to a man like the breasts in a woman. During the Jāgrata avasthā, merit and demerit are postulated of this Deva (power); he is capable of great expansion and is the inner

7

mover. He is Khaga, (bird), Karkata (crab), Puṣkara (ākāś), prāṇa, pain, parāpara, Ātmā and Bramha n. This deity causes to know.

He who knows thus obtains Bramha n, the supreme, the support of all things, and the Kṣetrajña. He obtains Bramha n, the supreme, support of all things, and the Kṣetrajña. "The Pursuha has four seats—navel, heart, neck, and head. There Bramha n with the four feet specially shines. Those feet are jāgrata, svapna, suṣupti, and turya. In jāgrata he is Brahmā, in svapna Vishṇu, in suṣupti Rudra, and in turya the supreme Akṣara. He is Aditya, Viṣṇu, Īśvara, Puruṣa, prāṇa, jīva, agni, the resplendent. The Para-Bramha n shines in the midst of these. He is without manas, ear, hands, feet, and light. There the worlds are no worlds, Devas no Devas, Vedas no Vedas, sacrifices no sacrifices, mother no mother, father no father, daughter-in-law no daughter-in-law, hermits no hermits; so, one only Bramha n shines as different. In the Hṛdayākāś (ākāś in the heart) is the Cidākāś. That is Bramha n. It is extremely subtle. The Hṛdayākāś can be known. This moves in it. In Bramha n, everything is strung. Those who thus know the Lord know everything.

In him the Devas, the worlds, the Pitṛs and the Ṛṣis do not rule. He who has awakened knows everything. All the Devas are in the heart; in the heart are all the prāṇas: in the heart are prāṇa, jyotis and that three-plied holy thread. In the heart in Caitanya, it (prāṇa) is. Put on the yajñopavīta (holy thread), the supreme, the holy, which came into existence along with the Prajāpati, which gives long life and which is very excellent; let this give you strength and tejas. Those whose tuft of hair is jñāna, who are firmly grounded in jñāna, consider jñāna only as supreme. Jñāna is holy and excellent. He whose śikhā (tuft of hair) is jñāna like the śikhi (flame of agni)—he, the wise one, only wears a true śikhā; others wear a mere tuft of hair. Those brāhmaṇas and others who perform the ceremonies prescribed in the Vedas—they wear this thread only as a symbol of their ceremonies. Those who know the Vedas say that he only is a true brāhmaṇa who wears the śikhā of jñāna and whose yajñopavīta is the same (jñāna). This yajñopavīta (Yajña means Viṣṇu or sacrifice and Upavīta is that which surrounds; hence that which surrounds

Viṣṇu) is supreme and is the supreme refuge. He who wears that really knows—he only wears the sūtra, he is Yajña (Viṣṇu) and he only knows Yajña (Viṣṇu).

One God hidden in all things, pervades all things and is the Inner Life of all things. He awards the fruits of <u>karma</u>, he lives in all things, he sees all things without any extraneous help, he is the soul of all, there is nothing like him, He is the great wise one. He is the one doer among the many action-less objects. He is always making one thing appear as several (by <u>SankalpA</u>). Those wise men who see him in <u>buddhi</u>, they only obtain eternal peace.

Having made Ātmā as the (upper) <u>arani</u> (attritional piece of wood) and <u>Pranava</u> the lower arani, by constant practice of dhyāna one should see the concealed deity. As the oil in the sesamum seed, as the <u>ghee</u> in the curds, as the water in the rivers, and as the fire in the arani, so they who practise truth and austerities see Him in the buddhi.

As the spider throws out and draws into itself the threads, so the jīva goes and returns during the jāgrata and the svapna states. The heart is in the form of a closed lotus-flower, with its head hanging down; it has a hole in the top. Know it to be the great abode of All.

Know that during jāgrata it (jīva) dwells in the eye, and during svapna in the throat; during suṣupti, it is in the heart and during turya in the head. (Because buddhi unites) the Pratyag-ātma with the Paramātma, the worship of <u>sandhyā</u> (union) arose. So, we should perform sandhyāvandana (rites).

The sandhyāvandana performed by dhyāna requires no water. It gives no trouble to the body or the speech. That which unites all things is the sandhyā of the one-staffed (sannyāsins). Knowing That from which speech and mind turn back without being able to obtain it and That which is the bliss of Jīva, the wise one is freed.

From Bramha Vidya Upanishad: (Swamini Vimalananda's notes)

Desire is the root cause of all knowledge, action and thinking. We believe that success is to achieve all we desire. Yet most of us do not succeed in fulfilling most of our desires, despite sincere efforts.

The eighth chapter of the Chandogya <u>Upanishad</u> drives home the fact that a state of total fulfilment of desires (Satya kama) is attained through **Bramha Vidya - the knowledge of Truth,** that results in Self-realization followed by realisation of Bramha m within us, whereby one remains untouched by any situation in life.

Indra, the king of heaven lived for 101 years in the hermitage of Prajapati, the Creator, in order to gain this knowledge and experience. A life of Self-control and meditation on the heart-space was the means taught, and total freedom and fulfilment, (the goal) was achieved. Desire is the root of all knowledge, action and thinking. It is the cause of our entire Samsara with all its grief, stress and strain.

Yet all of us seek only to fulfil our desires. We believe that freedom is to be able to do what we want, i.e., fulfil all our desires. Success is to achieve all we desire and happiness is to enjoy all we desired. Rather than seeking a state of desire-lessness, we wish to attain a state wherein we can fulfil all that we desire. And therefore, we are envious of people who have everything they desire? We feel attracted to and worship those who can produce and attain anything by mere will or wish? We daydream of indulging and gorging on all we desire? Would it not be wonderful if all we wanted came to us without us having to lift our little finger?

Such a state of fulfilment of desires (Satya KAma, Satya Sankalpa) is promised to us by the Scriptures and the wise through Self-realization. The Self is infinite and infinity alone is Bliss (Bhumaiva sukham). All objects and pleasures are included in the infinite Self and therefore Self-realization is a state of fulfilment of all desires. (According to Sri. RamAnujA this is step-1, and further one must realise the absolute truth or reality, the Bramha n, ultimate through one of the Bramha Vidyas) However, mere intellectual knowing does not result in Self-realization.

Being already one with us, Self-realization is not possible through any or many worldly actions or spiritual practices. Then how do we attain it?

One must meditate on it to realize it. Is meditation difficult? Can one meditate without a religious background? Is there any universal symbol of the Self/Truth that all can identify with? How long does it take? Is the practice interesting or tedious? 'I' am the centre of my life and of supreme interest to myself. Others may be indifferent to me, but my entire world revolves around me and 'I' alone am the focus of all my thoughts and efforts. Hence, meditation on the Self would seem quite natural and effortless. But that is not so. The pure Self, nameless and formless, (the AtmA) is extremely subtle and therefore a symbol or support is required to help our extroverted mind to refocus. The heart-space within, which is always available as 'here and now', is a universal symbol of the Self. Anyone irrespective of their religion, nationality, caste, creed or cline can meditate on it. Such meditation leads to Self- realization and a state of fulfilment of all desires. (This is one such Bramha Vidya- advised by Upanishad.)

However, such meditation is possible only for one, who is self-controlled, can manage one's mind and senses, and is able to sublimate one's Vasanas- impressions of pleasure and pain practiced and etched in our psyche over lifetimes. Control over even the most basic instincts like sex and other such compulsive and instinctive impressions render the mind subtle, pure, and focused, so that one can meditate on the Self. **Strange, but true indeed, that the control of desires is the means recommended to ultimately attain a state of total fulfilment of desires! This is the very theme of the eighth chapter of the Chandogya Upanishad.**

The Chandogya Upanisad forms part of the Bramha na-s of the Talavakara section of the Sama Veda. Like all Upanisad-s, its main topic is the Knowledge of the Truth (Bramha Vidya). However, the first five chapters mainly describe a variety of rituals (karma-s) and methods of worship and meditation (Upasana) catering to different types of people. The last three chapters predominantly propound Self-knowledge.

This Upanisad introduces us to endearing and earnest seekers of Truth like Narada, Satyakama and Svetaketu and compassionate teachers like Aruni, Sanatkumara and Prajapati. The stories and dialogues between different Guru-s and disciples teach us many important lessons of life.

In chapter VIII, one learns from Indra, sincerity and the patience required to gain great goals.

In the sixth chapter, through the story of Sage Uddalaka and his disciple-son, Shvetaketu, it was shown that the Truth alone really exists. Existence alone is the Truth and that Existence alone is the True Nature. All the names and forms experienced are only modifications superimposed on the Truth. The Truth is subtle and difficult to comprehend.

In the seventh chapter the Truth is indicated through the various superimposed modifications progressing gradually from the gross to the subtle. Finally, one realizes the Truth, which is beyond the gross and the subtle and designated here as Bramha n-the Infinite. This chapter also takes us through a range of meditations from the gross to the subtle thereby making us fit for meditation on the highest Truth.

In the final chapter of the Chandogya Upanishad, Prajapati, the Creator, promises agelessness, fearlessness, immortality, total freedom, and fulfilment of all desires through Self-realization. The Self is available 'here and now' to one and all and it is to be meditated upon in the 'heart-space' within.

> **Self-knowledge**
>
> The all pervading Atman,
> Like butter concealed in milk,
> In self-knowledge, self-discipline rooted,
> Is the final goal of the Upanishad.

We find herein the story of Indra, the king of heaven attaining realization after living for 101 long years, a life of self-control spent in study, reflection, and meditation; and Virochana, the king of demons, living for 32 years, misunderstanding the knowledge, and spreading a materialistic and selfish doctrine.

This clearly shows the importance of a pure and subtle mind and the means to achieve it for Self-realization.

5. Prajapati Vakyam

Bramha Vidya in Bagavat Gita as stated by Sri. Alawandar (One of Sri. RamAnujA's Guru) and Sri. RamaNujA. (Prajapati Vakyam from Gitartha Sangragam and Kalakshepam of Vaikuntavasi Sri. Mannarkudi Rajagopalan, AstAna Vidvan of Sri Ahobila Mutt)

Bagavat Sri. Ramanujar   Sri. Alawandar

तदेवं मुमुक्षुभिः प्राप्यतया वेदान्तोदित-निरस्तनिखिल अविद्यादिदोषगन्द अननधिकातिशय असंख्येय कल्याणगुणगण परब्रह्मपुरुषोत्तम प्राप्त्युपायभूत-वेदनोपासनध्यानादि शब्दवाच्य (वाच्यां) तदैकान्तिकात्यन्तिकभक्तिं वक्तुं तदङ्गभूतम् "आत्माऽपहतपाप्मा"(छा.८.७.१)। इत्यादिप्रजापतिवाक्योदितं प्राप्तुरात्मनो याताम्यदर्शनं तन्नित्यताज्ञानपूर्वक असङ्गकर्म निष्ठाद्यज्ञानयोगसाध्यमुक्तम् ।

tadēvam̐ mumukṣubhiḥ prāpyatayā vēdāntōdita- nirastanikhila avidyādidōṣaganda anavadhikātiśaya asam̐khyēya kalyāṇaguṇagaṇa paraBramha puruṣōttama prāptyupāyabhūta - vēdanōpāsanadhyānādi śabdavācya (vācyam̐) tadaikāntikātyantikabhaktim̐ vaktum̐ taṅgabhūtam
"ātmā'pahatapāpmā"(chā.8.7.1). *ityādiprajāpativākyōditam̐ prāpturātmanō yātāmyadarśanam̐ tannityatajñānapūrvaka asaṅgakarma niṣṣādyajñānayōgasādhyamuktam |*

Discussions on the PrajApati Vakyam:

Two questions arise in our mind when we read this long sentence.
1.How, what is stated to Arjuna to fight, is applicable to common men like us?
2.How Atma yatatmyam (Atma ShatcatkAram) spoken here (Avara PurushArtam) is applicable to Mumukshus. Is it not that, Parama PurushArtam is to "reach BhagavAn Tiruvadi for Mumukshus". (VishishtAdvaita Philosophy).

Bagavat RamAnujar answers both question in detail in 3rd chapter AvatArikai- of Bagavat GitA

What is stated to Arjuna is not ParamAtmA's Udyeshyam. (Intention) It is only a Vyajyam. (Excuse). In LoukikA what is done for one reason, after the reason is over still continued for Loka Shemam as stated in Bramha SutrA. Similarly, here, even though ArjunA is given Upadesam, it is meant for all of us only.

"Atma YatAtmyam" is an **Angabutam** for realising Bhagavan and that in itself is not PurushArtham.

Both Lord Krishna and Bagavat RamAnujA are trying to say that Gita ShAstram is advocating Bhakti.

And, Bakti **alone** can lead to Bramha m and so, with Love and affection one has to do Bhakti to Him. Swami AlawandAr's summary relating to the entire GitaShAstram is shown in his first slokA of GitArtha Sangragam:

स्वधर्मज्ञानवैराग्यसाध्य भक्त्येक गोचरः |

नारायणः परं ब्रह्म गीता शास्त्रे समीरितः||

svadharmajñānavairāgyasādhyabhaktyēkagōcaraḥ |
nārāyaṇaḥ paraṁ Bramha gītā śāstrē samīritaḥ |

(Alawandar-Gitartha Sangraga: slokA-1)

Gita ShAstram is a granta which tells about Bhakti, and Bramha m is Upayam and Upeyam also. (The goal and means) This Bhakti Yoga's Angam is first taught since it is a must to attain His feet, only after realising the **PatyagAtma-** (one's self AtmA) the AngA. This in itself is not a PurushArtam and only a (ladder) step to go up.

Now let us see the full meaning of the sloka mentioned above:

तदेवं मुमुक्षुभिः प्राप्यतया वेदान्तोदित-निरस्तनिखिल अविद्यादिदोषगन्द अनवधिकातिशय

असंख्येय कल्याणगुणगण परब्रह्मपुरुषोत्तम प्राप्त्युपायभूत-वेदनोपासनध्यानादि शब्दवाच्य

(वाच्यां) तदैकान्तिकात्यन्तिकभक्तिं वक्तुं तदङ्गभूतम् "आत्माऽपहतपाप्मा"(छा.८.७.१)।

इत्यादिप्रजापतिवाक्योदितं प्राप्रुरात्मनो यातात्म्यदर्शनं तन्नित्यताज्ञानपूर्वक असङ्गकर्म

निष्ठाद्यज्ञानयोगसाध्यमुक्तम् ।

Mumuchubhi: - Those who want to get out of SamsAram and do kainkaryam
(service) to Bramha m in sarvadesa, sarva kAla, and sarvavastai. These persons
also do kainkaryam to Bramha m, in SamsArA. For them what is stated in VedA
as PrApyam? Acquirable-i.e., where one must go, which is acquirable by them.

Sri. RamAnujA describes the Bramha m's Lakshanam. (Bramha m is the goal
and it is also the means (Route to reach the same).

निरस्तनिखिल अविद्यादिदोषगन्द अनवधिकातिशय असंख्येय कल्याणगुणगण परब्रह्मपुरुषोत्तम

प्राप्त्युपायभूत

*nirastanikhila avidyādidōṣaganda anavadhikātiśaya asaṁkhyēya kalyāṇaguṇagaṇa
paraBramha puruṣōttama prāptyupāyabhūta.*

Bramha m (Sriman NarAyaNA) is unrelated to Avidya dosha etc., (**Dosha
Sambandha Anarhan-DoshA never touches Him**) and Iis KalyANa GuNA
are, SwAbAgitvam, (Natural), without any limit, countless, and having Ananda
Roopam.

He is addressed as परब्रह्मपुरुषोत्तम- **ParaBramha n and PurushOtaman** by Sri.
RamAnujA to cover what is stated by both Shruti and Smruti about the supreme
reality. ParaBramha is objective name and NarAyaNa is subjective name.
PurushOtaman is objective name and Vasudeva is subjective name. He is PrApti
UpAyam for Mumukshus. i.e., He is the route-(means) to PrApti for
Mumukshus.

6. PrajApati Vakyam- Sri. RamAnujA's explanation

PRAJAPATI VAKYAM- SRI. RAMANUJA'S EXPLANATION ESTABLISHES BRAMHA VIDYA CLEARLY

What should a Mumuks hu do	With desire to leave SamsArA and reach Bramha m's Tiruvadi he must desire and work.	तदेवं मुमुक्षुभिः	tadēvaṁ mumukṣ ubhiḥ
Who is Bramha m?	Sriman NARAyan A.	परब्रह्म (Vaidikam) पुरुषोत्तम (Loukikam)	paraBramha puruṣ ōttama (Refer above for details)
Who says so?	Refer Sri. Alawandar 's sloka above given under GitArtha Sangragam	स्वधर्मज्ञानवैराग्यसाध्य भक्त्येक गोचरः। नारायणः परं ब्रह्म गीता शास्त्रे समीरितः।।	svadharmajñānavairāgyasādhyabhakty ēkagōcaraḥ। nārāyaṇaḥ paraṁ Bramha gītā śāstrē samīritaḥ। (Alawandar Gitartha Sangraga: slokA-1)
What are th Bramha m' Lakshanan	KalyANa guNA	निरस्तनिखिल अविद्यादिदोषगन्द अनवधिकातिशय असंख्येय कल्याणगुणगण, प्राप्त्युपायभूत	nirastanikhila avidyādidōṣ aganda anavadhikātiśaya asaṁkhyēya kalyāṇaguṇagaṇa, prāptyupāyabhūta
How does a Mumuks	With desire to leave SamsArA, and reach	वेदनोपासनध्यानादि शब्दवाच्य (वाच्यां)	vēdanōpāsanadhyānādi śabdavācya (vācyaṁ)

hu reach Him?	Bramham's Tiruvadi he must carry out with Bakti (Love and affection) Vedana, or Dhyanam, or UpAsanam of that single object.		
What are the qualities of Bhakti?	Ekantam- By object or PrayojanA (Use) it is Para-Bramha m only, and no one else. (Nirnayam - concluded) Second is always Atyantika- Sarva kAla VyApyam (applicable). This Bhakti on NarAyaN A cannot change with time.	तदैकान्तिकात्यन्तिकभक्तिं वक्तुं	tadaikāntikātyantikabhaktiṁ vaktuṁ
Is this Bhakti and UpAsana sufficient or some more things	PratyagAt ma SAtcAtkA ram is a must	तदङ्गभूतम् "आत्माऽपहतपाप्मा"(छा .८.७.१)	taṅgabhūtam "ātmā'pahatapāpmā"(chā.8.7.1).

| Who says so? And when? | PrajApati to DevA king IndrA When Indra sticks to PrajApati and asks questions for route to Liberation. | इत्यादिप्रजापतिवाक्यो दितं प्रासुरात्मनो याताम्यदर्शनं तन्नित्यताज्ञानपूर्वक असङ्गकर्म निष्षाद्यज्ञानयोगसाध्य मुक्तम् | ityādiprajāpativākyōditaṁ prāpturātmanō yātāmyadarśanaṁ tannityatājñānapūrvaka asaṅgakarma niṣ ṣ ādyajñānayōgasādhyamuktam |

What is advocated in VedA to attain the Bramham?

वेदनोपासनध्यानादि शब्दवाच्य (वाच्यां), **vēdanōpāsanadhyānādi śabdavācya (vācyāṁ)** i.e., Vedanam (Meditation), UpAsanam, and DhyAnam. All the three are one and the same and so, they are shown separately here. These three are VAcaka sabdham and Bakti is VAchya Sabdham. By following any one of them. तदैकान्तिकात्यन्तिकभक्तिं वक्तुं, **tadaikāntikātyantikabhaktiṁ vaktuṁ.** Bakti has two adjectives here. One is **Ekantam**- By object or PrayojanA (Use) Bakti to be expressed to **Para-Bramha m** only and no one else. (Antam-Nirnayam-concluded). Second is **Atyantika**- Sarva kAla VyApyam (applicable). This Bakti is not one time, but continued till one leave this earth.

Before getting such a Bhakti to realise Bramha m, **Sri. RamAnujA** says realising and knowing about Self's AtmA is a must as per **PrajApati Vakyam, in Chandokya Upanishad (8.7.1).** वक्तुं "आत्माऽपहतपाप्मा"(छा.८.७.१)। **vaktuṁ "ātmā'pahatapāpmā"(chā.8.7.1).** आत्माऽपहतपाप्मा − refers to a JivA without DoshA. JivA incidentally when attaining MokshA, gets SAmyam with Bramha m for enjoying all the pleasures (Bogams) which He enjoys. Other than Sriyapatitvam, Capacity to make Shrushti and able to give MokshA to JivA, one gets Samyam with Bramha m after attaining MokshA.

By this PrajApati's vAkyam, "आत्माऽपहतपाप्मा"(छा.८.७.१), to IndrA who came to PrajApati and asked him to give Upadesam of **"Self-realisation"** it is established that by carrying out Atma ShAtcAtkAram, **whoever wants Moksham (liberation)**, gets GjAnam (ज्ञानम्) about Bramha n, as a first step, and by Vedana, or Dhyana, or Upasana of that Bramha m, one could then attain MokshA as step-2. *(See also Section 13. Conclusion)*

7. Bramha Vidya according to Wikipedia

Bramha vidya is that branch of scriptural knowledge derived primarily through a study of the Upanishads, Bramha -Sutras and Bhagavat Gita, and derived from the Sanskrit words Bramha and Vidyā.

Bramha m is the neuter gender of the root word-form "brih" that means big. As the word big has not been further qualified to reveal its dimension, we must understand that Bramha m, the word means that which is free from all forms of limitation.

The word VidyA is derived from the root (Dhatu-in Sanskrit) vid- to know or to learn. To know or learn about Bramha m, only that which helps us to escape, the cycle of birth and death, and attain the feet of the Shrushti Kartha, the Bramha m is VidyA (**Sa VidyA Vimuktaye**) and other learnings or knowledge is only a Loukika Vishayam. (Knowing worldly matters).

Bramha vidya is the spiritual knowledge of the Absolute Truth or Reality or Bramha m according to Bramha -SutrA. Vidya is the highest ideal of classical Sanatana Dharma taught to anyone. Bramha -Vidya does not pertain only to Sanatana Dharma, as many other faiths practice and learn Bramha vidya through different means; Each faith teaches about the divine through different studies, yet the Bramha -Vidya is one and the same – **Truth the Reality itself.**

In the Puranas, this is divided into two branches, the first one dealing with the Vedic mantras and is called Para Vidya or 'former knowledge', and the latter dealing with the study of the Upanishads and is called the Apara-vidya or 'latter knowledge'. Both para- and Apara-vidya constitute Bramha -Vidya. The Mundaka Upanishad says that **"Bramha -vidya sarva-vidya pratistha"**, which means "The Knowledge of Bramha n (that which is Bramha is Bramha n) is the foundation of all knowledge."

Bramha -mimamsa is a masterly treatise, weighty and illuminating, summing up the Dvaita standpoint in Vedanta by Dharmadhikari Prof., H N Raghanvendrachar, M A., D.O.C., for benefit of readers intrested in Madhvacharya's Dvaita Philosophy.

DhyanA, Meditation and UpAsanA

These three are one and the same. While **meditation** is an English word, **DhyanA** is a Sanskrit word both meaning same. UpAsanA is again a Sanskrit word meaning worship and service. Vedanta Sutras define Upasana as enquiry into Bramha n. It does not stop there. It is study, Investigation, and reasoning, contemplation, and meditation. Thus, Meditation is long and continued meditation.

8. Adhikari Vishesham, Sources and Knowledge of Bramham through a Guru

Adhikari Vishesham (Eligibility) for Meditation

A person who is knowledgeable enough to realise that he should act in this Birth itself, to put an end to the cycle of births and deaths becomes eligible for Upasana. It is such a person's love and affection towards Bramha m, that he focuses on Bramha n, constantly by meditation. This should not be construed to hinder in daily life, because the daily duties themselves are to be carried out in a spirit of worship of the Lord and with three thyagas namely Kartrutva, Mamata and Phala. (**Kartrutva**- "I" am doing, **Mamata**- Actions and results are Mine, **Phala**- Fruits of actions)

Sources for Bramha Vidya

Upanishads, Vedanta Sutras or Bramha Sutras, and Bhagavat Gita.

In Upanishads, the focus on Bramha Vidya is more under, Chandokya, Bruhadaranyaka, and Taitreeya. Other Upanishads which deal with Bramha Vidya are, Kata Upanishad, Kaushcetaki Upanishad, Prasnopanishad, Isavasya Upanishad and Mundaka Upanishad. Some minor changes in numbers are there in the Bramha Vidya. Ramanuja says 32 and Sankara says 30. It does not matter because anyone can choose any Vidya for doing Upasana.

Bramha sutra BhAshyam under chapter three, Padha three, details of Bramha Vidya are dealt with and we will see below the BhAshyam of Sri. RamAnujA briefly. In the introduction of the book, Mundaka and Mandukya Upanishad published by Ramkrishna math, Mylapore, Madras in 1920 and authored by Swami Sharvananda, it is stated that:

The Mundaka Upanishad says that "Bramha -vidya sarva-vidya pratistha", which means **"The Knowledge of Bramha n is the foundation of all knowledge."** The book also says that since reference to Mundaka is taken in the name, and Mundaka meaning razor, and shaving head fully, this is more appropriate for Sanyasins than Grahasta.

Knowledge of Bramha m through a Guru

In Sanatana Dharma, Philosophy, all ascetic leaders advocate, the Ultimate goal for the self is Realising Self (Atma), and Bramha n as one and the same. But understanding of Self (Atma) or Bramha n is a process **guided through a Guru,** who himself has gone through this process of learning from his Guru and reached a stage where he could guide others. All our Scriptures, are therefore always in the form of a Question-and-Answer format only. The Questioner is a great scholar or person, or a King of repute and the Guru is equally or more well versed with knowledge and have experienced to answer their query.

Two, examples are stated here to understand this point: Mahabharat and Ramayana are two Epics (Iti-hasa, this is how it happened), and heroes of both, Yudhistra, and Arjuna, (from Mahabharata) and Rama (from Ramayana) had doubts on purpose of life, and as Kings how they must administer the Kingdom?

Therefore, they asked questions: Yudhistra and Arjuna to Lord Krishna and Rama to Vashishtar. Resultant GranthAs were, **Sri Vishnu Sahasranamam,** (Anushasana Parva Section 149) Bhagavat Gita (does not need any further reference) and **Yoga Vashishtam** (Rama when brought to the Palace for getting instruction from his father to go and help Rishi Viswamittirar at forest, looking at his sadness, Viswamittirar requested Rishi Vashishtar to give him Upadesam about **Paramartika Gjanam,** (ज्ञानम्) (knowledge about Bramha n.) The details of questions and answers and what we must follow are all brought out in these Granthas and it would be helpful to understand and lead life according to the advice given in these Grantas, to attain the purpose of Manushya JanmA and to remain happy.

These **Thirty-two VidyAs** are listed below and each one teaches a specific quality(swaroopam) of Bramha n on which a Sadaka is supposed to focus constantly and regularly, while carrying out Upasana to achieve liberation. It is also added in this Table extracts from a Tamil book written and published by Dr. Venkatesh MBBs., CCEBDM, MBA. He is a ShishyA of Villur NadAdur, Sri Bhashya SimhAsanam, SAstra SAhitee, Vallaba Vidvanmani, Dr. Sri. MatuPayave, KarunAkarArya Maha Desikan. The name of the book is **Sri Vidyaigalum and Sri. Rajagopalnum** (ஸ்ரீவித்யைகளும்ஸ்ரீ ராஜகோபாலனும்.), (மன்னார்குடி ஸ்ரீராஜகோபாலன் செய்தருளியலீலைகளும், அவை

உணர்த்தும் உபநிஷத் ப்ரஹ்ம வித்யைகளும்). All LeelAs done by BhagavAn Sri. Mannarkudi Rajagopalan and the way they indicate Upanishad Bramha VidyAs.

9. Bramha -Vidya Names

Sr No	Name of the Vidya	Which Upanishad?	What to concentrate in this Vidya	Mannarkudi Rajagopalan Leela.32 Vidyas are shown by Baghavan Kannan to Gopralaya Rishis
1	GAyatri VidyA	Bramha n as the Holy Gayatri Mantra	Chandokya Upanishad, III. xii	**Leelais: GopAlan one who mends Cows.** If we do DhyanA of his effulgence, He would control our mind from wandering and stabilise the same as Cows were mended by Him.
2	Aksi(अक्षि) VidyA	Bramha n as being present within the Eye	Chandokya Upanishad, IV.xv.1	**Kannan with flute SevA.** Three qualities said in this VidyA, on which to do UpAsanA is shown by Kannan. 1.One who keeps likable objects with Him (SamyAtvAma:) 2.VAmanee: Gives all benefits to those who surrender to Him. 3.Bhamanee: One who has effulgence.
3	AksharAkshara Vidya **(Akshara-Para)**	Meditation on the Imperishable	Mundaka Upanishad, I	**SevA:** सर्वज्ञन्-यसर्वज्ञस्सर्वविद्यस्य ज्ञानमयं तप: One who knows everything clearly by Swaroopam and PrakAram. He made DuryOdanA to stand when He entered the Rajya Sabha. He showed **Sarvagjatvam(सर्वज्ञत्वम्)** in this episode.
4	AkAsha VidyA	Making sound and through AkAsha reaches to us.	Chandokya Upanishad-1	**Udgita Sound, though Flute,** by Uth-One who is supreme. Since AkAsha brings all sounds, in this VidyA, ParamAtmA brings this **Utgita** sound to all of us through flute.
5	Sadh-VidyA	Bramha n as the ground of all being	Chandokya Upanishad, VI	**VatsApaharaNa sEvA**-During PralayA He alone existed and other Cetana, Acetana (all of them were within Him without name and form). Later after He makes SankalpA to become many they get names and forms. This essence of Sad VidyA was shown by Kannan to Gopralaya Rishis.
6	AntarAdithya VidyA	Bramha n as the Inner Controller of the Sun	Chandokya Upanishad, I.vi.6	AntarAdithya VidyA says to do DhyanA of Bramha n, **at the center of Surya Mandalam, and with brightness of Gold.** Along with Rukmini, and SatyabhAmA on his crown He sat and gave darshan to Gopralaya Rishis.
7	Bhooma VidyA	Bramha n as the Great One	Chandokya Upanishad, VII	Sridevi, Bhudevi sameda **Para Vasudeva sEvA** to Gopralaya Rishis. Bhuma vidya keeps saying one by one which is better than what and finally

Sr No	Name of the Vidya	Which Upanishad?	What to concentrate in this Vidya	Mannarkudi Rajagopalan Leela.32 Vidyas are shown by Baghavan Kannan to Gopralaya Rishis
				says Satyam- the ParamAtmA is better than everyone. This is explained by Bahu+MA- Better than every vastu. Keeping this in mind one h to do DhyanA of Him as recommended by Bhuma VidyA.
8	Madhu VidyA	Bramha n as Honey	Chandokya Upanishad, III. i	**Shining in like SuryA**-Without UdayA (rising) and AstamaNA (To go away) ParaBramha m is always shining in like SuryA as stated in this VidyA. This sEvA was shown to Yashoda when He drank milk from her Breast.
9	Purusha VidyA	Milkman SevA to show that milk is important for YagA and JivA's life itself is a YagA.	Chandokya Upanishad, III. 16,17	**Milk man** -पुरुष वाव यज्ञः This VidyA says the life of a Jiva itself is a YAgA. Since the life itself is depicted as a YagA, He takes the form of a milk man and showed milk is an important Dravyam for YagA.
10	SarvAntarAtm aVidyA	BhagavAn is AntarAtmA for everyone.	Brahadaranya m Upanishad-111-7	**Vatsa-KapitsAsura Vadam**-यं पृथिवी न वेद, यस्य पृथिवी शरीरं, यः पृथिवीं अन्तरो यमयति, in this VidyA, starts like this and says Earth, water, Agni (Fire) and AkAsham all are His shareeram and He remains within them as **AntarAtmA.** Further He even stays inside JivA is stated in this Upanishad. य आत्मनि तिष्ठन्, आत्मनो ऽन्तरः, यमात्मा न वेद, यस्यआत्माशरीरं, यआत्मानं अन्तरो यमयति, एष त आत्मा अन्तर्याम्यमृतः
11	VysvAnara VidyA	Bramha n as the Universal Being. Viswaroopa Darshanam	Chandokya Upanishad, V. xi	**GitAUpadesam-Viswaroopa Darshanam.** VysvAnara Vidya describes the **Viswaroopa Darshanam as follows:** तस्यह्वाएतस्यातमनःड
12	PanchAgni VidyA	The Meditation of the Five Fires	Chandokya Upanishad, V. iii to x.	A JivA's **sookshama ShreerA** along with PrANA and Senses (IndriyA) is first joined with "Swarga Agni." Second is "Megam Agni". Third in "Bhumi Agni. "Fourth into mens" shareerA. Last and fifth is Stree's shareerA, stays there for ten months and then born in this earth. Therefore, it becomes a PancAgni VidyA. Similar to giving Ahuti with DravyA in Agni, if one gives his AtmA in PancAgni He will take the JivA to Moksha through ArchirAdi Gati. Since **ButanA, gave her milk from Stanam, having kept it as**

Sr No	Name of the Vidya	Which Upanishad?	What to concentrate in this Vidya	Mannarkudi Rajagopalan Leela.32 Vidyas are shown by Baghavan Kannan to Gopralaya Rishis
				ArpaNam to Him only she attained MokshA.
13	Dahara VidyA	Bramha n as the Imperceptible Ether within the Heart	Chandokya Upanishad, VIII	**Rukmani, SatyabHAma Sri Rajagopalan SevA.** Dahara Vidya advocates, a UpAsakan's ShareerA as Bramha puram, (Bramha m's place of residence), and the Lotus at the center of the Heart as His residence, shrinking all His greatness, Bramha m resides in the small place inside heart of a JivA. That Bramha m is to be searched and found. Dahara Vidya says find out such a Bramha n inside you.
14	PrAna VidyA	Bramha n as the Vital Breath	Chandokya Upanishad, I.xi.5	**SevA in Haridra River in Mannarkudi,** along with GopikA (jalakridA). PrAna. This Vidya explains PrAna's greatness and explains the method to do UpAsanaA of Bramha m, residing within that PrAna as AntarAtmA. The way we cannot live without PrAna, GopikAs showed they cannot live with their PrAnanAthan Kannan.
15	NachiketAgni VidyA	Meditation with the Naciketa fire	Katha Upanishad, I. ii	**NachketAgni.** NachiketA goes to the God of death's place. (Yamadharma RajA's kingdom). NachiketA gets three boons from YamA out of which second boon is "NachketA's query about Agni which takes to SwargA (Here SwargA is MokshA) YamA also gave him a boon and named the second Agni as NachketAgni. Meditation on that Agni leads to SwargA to be understood as Liberation.
16	Upakosala VidyA	Meditation as taught to Upakosala-	Chandokya Upanishad, IV. x	**Rukmani-SatyabhAmA sevA and listening to flute songs.** कं ब्रह्म खं ब्रह्म. कं is bliss and खं is limitless. This shows that Bramha m is without limits, and like AkAshA limitless with AnandA. It is to show that limitless AnandA he gave SevA to us as **Rukmani-SatyabhAmA sameda GopAlan listening to flute.**
17	SatyakAma VidyA	Meditation as taught to Satyakaama Jaabaala	Chandokya Upanishad, IV. iv	In this Vidya, Bramha m showed four different SevA to a person named SatyakAman as Bull or Ox, Agni, Annam, and a Bird named Madugu. In this each one said how Bramha m looks. Bullock said Bramha m have four different RoopA. First one Bull said, having East, West, South and North direction within Bramha m.

Sr No	Name of the Vidya	Which Upanishad?	What to concentrate in this Vidya	Mannarkudi Rajagopalan Leela.32 Vidyas are shown by Baghavan Kannan to Gopralaya Rishis
				Second, Agni said, Buloka, SwarlogA, Antariksha LogA and Ocean within Bramha m. Third, an Annam said, Agni, Sun, Chandran, Lightening within Bramha m. Fourth and last a bird said, PrANA, Eyes, ears, and Manas within Bramha m. In this way just as Bramha m is divided into four different forms and shown to SatyakAman, Kannan showed to GopikAs four different forms as **YamA to Boxers, King, for GopikA and PrajA, and all three in one form to Gopila GopralayA.**
18	IsAvAshya VidyA	Govardhana Giri dHari sEvA	IsAvAshya (ईशावास्य) SlokA-II	**GovardhanaGiri dHari sEvA** ईशावास्यं इदं सर्वम्. Kannan said to Ayars (ஆயர்கள்) that He resides in everything in this Universe, and so, do PoojA to Govardhana Giri. He was inside the Giri as AntaryAmi and took that PoojA. Also, this Upanishad teaches NishkAmya karma. He stopped Ayars from doing Indra PoojA and made them do PoojA to Govardhana Giri as an angam of His tiruvArAdhaNa कुर्वन्नेवेह कर्माणि जिजीविषेत् शतं समाः । एवं त्वयि नान्यथेतोऽस्ति न कर्म लिप्यते नरे ॥
19	Samvarga VidyA	The entire Universe inside His mouth to YashOdhA.	Chandokya Upanishad, IV. iii	**The entire Universe inside His mouth to YashOdhA** Vayu and PrANA, both are shareerA for Bramha m is shown. In this way Sun, Moon, Agni, Eyes, Ears, and Manas everything is within Bramha m is seen by YashOdhA. By opening His mouth and showing her the entire Universe, the point is everything is within Him.
20	Gargi-Akshara VidyA	Bramha n as the support for everything.	Brhadaaranya ka Upanishad, III.viii.8	**With stick in His hand, he is mending all Cows SevA.** Yagjnyavalkar says to Gargi, Bramha m which is support (AdhAram) for everything is named as Aksharam, in this VidyA. एतद्वै तदक्षरं गार्गी ब्राह्मणा अभिवदन्ति. Further Yagjnyavalkar says to Gargi, that only due to His (Bramha m) SankalpA Sun, Moon, Bhumi, and AkAshA are all carrying out their KarmA-actions in their respective places. This is shown by Kannan with stick in His hand and mending all the

Sr No	Name of the Vidya	Which Upanishad?	What to concentrate in this Vidya	Mannarkudi Rajagopalan Leela.32 Vidyas are shown by Baghavan Kannan to Gopralaya Rishis
				Cows. By seeing the stick only, they all move, and by this He showed that entire Universe do their activity only by His sankalpA.
21	Bhrugu-Varuni VidyA	Meditation as taught by the god Varuna	Taittiriya Upanishad, Bhriguvalli	**Kannan as child crawling to YashOdhA SevA.** Bhrugu Muni asks VaruNA, to make him know Bramha m. VaruNA replied him to start thinking with his Intellect and know Him. Bhrugu also did the same and Taitreeya Upanishad says, finally Bhrugu understood that Bramha m is Ananda Roopam. (प्राणो ब्रह्मेति व्यजानात्, मनो ब्रह्मेति व्यजानात्, आनन्दं ब्रह्मेति व्यजानात्)
22	Anandamaya-VidyA	Bramha n as the Self consisting of Bliss	Taittiriya Upanishad, Anandavalli	**Playing with GopikA in a park with extreme happiness SevA.** Bramha m's Anandam is one hundred times more than Bramha , but it continues to say with our Manas we cannot understand the same. The essence of Ananda maya VidyA as per Anandavalli in Taitreeya Upanishad is not only He enjoys, but makes His BhaktA also equally enjoy.
23	AngushtamAtra-VidyA	Bramha n as resident within the Heart, of individual, of the size of Thumb	Katha Upanishad, II.iv.12	Even though, Bramha m is boundary and limitless, He shrinks Himself **to the size of every individual AtmA's thumb size and present in their heart** for them to see and do UpAsanA says, KathA Upanishad. In order to show that He could shrink and show Himself to His BaktA, **He Himself got tied to Ural(உரல்) and shown His SevA to YashOdhA.** But the doshA in them does not touch Him and He also does not hate them because of their Asuddhi in ShareerA or DoshA. अङ्गुष्ठमात्रःपुरुषोमध्यआत्मनितिष्ठति। ईशानोभूतभव्यस्य न ततो विजुगुप्सते ॥
24	ShAndilya-VidyA	Meditation as taught by Sandilya	Chandokya Upanishad, III.xiv.7	**Bramha m shows Himself differently to those who are proud and those who are having Bakti with affection to Him.** When He is inside our heart, He is even smaller than 1/100th of the tip of the paddy, but we know He is biggest of all (ब्रह्म). This is the essence of ShAndilya-VidyA. This is the SevA he showed to Rukmani satisfying Himself with a Tulsi Leaf and for SatyabhAmA even when She put all Her ornaments, did not allow the

Sr No	Name of the Vidya	Which Upanishad?	What to concentrate in this Vidya	Mannarkudi Rajagopalan Leela.32 Vidyas are shown by Baghavan Kannan to Gopralaya Rishis
				weighing scale to tilt in favour of ornaments.
25	Balaki -VidyA	Meditation as taught to Baalaaki	Kaushitaki Upanishad, IV	Kalia Nardhana SevA. Kalian thought Kannan was a child and surrounded his body and tried to kill Him. But when **Kannan, stood on Kalian's head**, he realised that He must be Bramha m Sriman NarAyaNA. Kaushitaki Upanishad teaches this Vidya यो वै बालाके एतेषां पुरुषाणां कर्ता, यस्य वैतत् कर्म, स वै वेदितव्यः that Bramha m is karthA and Cause for everything, and He is the one we must know. (**Vid-VidyA**). This Upanishad further says, if a JivA understands(knows) that Bramha m is the cause and KarthA for everything and does UpAsanA of Him, He removes all his KarmA and gives him Moksha (which is a higher state than a SamsAri and belongs to Bramha m)
26	Ushastha-Kahola-VidyA	Dancing child with butter on one hand.	Brhadaaranyaka Upanishad, II. iv, v	**Dancing child with butter on one hand SevA.** Essence of Ushastha-Kahola-VidyA is: We can also live with Anandam of a child, after attaining MokshA through Him, when we realise, and do UpAsanA of Him, that Bramha m is inside every Atma, similar to butter being inside Milk. एषत आत्मा सर्वान्तरोऽतोऽन्यदार्तम् तस्मात् ब्राह्मणः पाण्डित्यं निर्विद्य बाल्येन तिष्ठासेत्
27	Maitreyi-VidyA	Meditation as taught by Yajnavalkya to his wife Maitreyi	Brhadaaranyaka Upanishad, II. iv	Rukmani-SatyabhAmA sameda SevA Maitryi Vidya teaches, "आत्मा वा अरे द्रष्टव्यः श्रोतव्यो मन्तव्यो निदित्यासितव्यः" In this Vidya there are only **two commands**, which are one has **to see Bramha m as if he is seeing Him in person,** (द्रष्टव्यः) and carry out DhyAnam of Him (निदित्यासितव्यः) along with Rukmini and SatyabhAmA (single-as a Vishishta vidhi) as per our AchAryAs. Other vAkyams श्रोतव्यः, मन्तव्यः are not commands, since one who learns VedA will automatically listen to the same and

Sr No	Name of the Vidya	Which Upanishad?	What to concentrate in this Vidya	Mannarkudi Rajagopalan Leela.32 Vidyas are shown by Baghavan Kannan to Gopralaya Rishis
				think about it in mind. These are recitation or repetitions.
28	Parama-Purusha-VidyA	Bramha n as the Supreme Person. He is the means and He is the Goal also.	Katha Upanishad, I. iii	DasAvatAra sevA to DadhipAndavan, since he gave place to hide to Lord Krishna, when YashodA was running after Him to beat Him due to His stealing Curd. He requested Kannan, to give him mokshA as a pratiupakAram. **This VidyA teaches that DadhipAndavan, was not fit for UpAyam, the Bhakti YogA and so, Bramha m (Kannan) Himself stood as (UpAyam) means and gave him and his pot mokshA.** आत्मानं रथिनं विद्ध,शरीसं रथमेव च, बुद्धिं तु सारथीं विद्ध,मनः प्रग्रहं एव च, इन्द्रियाणि ह्यान् आहुः Bramha m is the ultimate goal a JivA has to attain and aim for is brought out in this VidyA. This Upanishad under Paramapurusha vidyA, says, AtmA as traveller in the chariot, body is chariot, Buddhi (intellect) is charioteer, Mind (manas) is bridle, and senses are horses. सोऽध्वनः पारमाप्नोति तद्विष्णोः परमं पदम्) Bramha m is the ultimate goal a JivA has to attain and aim for. सा काष्ठा सा परा गतिः Upanishad also says, the goal (Upeyam) and means (UpAyam) both are Bramha m only.
29	Paryanka-VidyA	Bramha n as the highest God seated in the Supreme Abode	Kaushitaki Upanishad, I	**SevA:** Kannan as MadanagopAlan, embraces all the GopikAs with affection and Love. In this VidyA it is stated that, those MuktAtmA who reach VaikuntA, Bramha m takes them in His lap, and give them Bramha nubhavam and limitless Anandam. This is the essence of this Paryanka VidyA also.
30	JyothishAmjyotir-VidyA	Bramha n as the Light of Lights	Brhadaaranyaka Upanishad, IV. iii.	**SevA:** Eating with GopikAs. अत्र पिताऽपिताभवति,माताऽमाता,लोकाऽलोका,देवाऽदेवाः GopikAs, forgetting their parents, residence, and city and in stoon stage enjoy and eat with Bramha m, (Kannan). In this vidyA, Rishi, Yagjnyavalkar

Sr No	Name of the Vidya	Which Upanishad?	What to concentrate in this Vidya	Mannarkudi Rajagopalan Leela.32 Vidyas are shown by Baghavan Kannan to Gopralaya Rishis
				teaches King JanakA, about JivA, uniting with Bramha m in sleeping state. This VidyA explains, the JivA in sleeping state as follows: प्राज्ञेनात्मना संपरिष्वक्तो न बाह्यं किंचन वेद नान्तरम्। तद्वाअस्यैतदासकाममात्मकाममकामँरूपँ शोकान्तरम् ॥ During the sleeping state of JivA, the Bramha m embraces him and makes him not to have any sorrow and keeps him in a state of Anandam (Bliss)
31	NyAsa-VidyA	Self-surrender to Bramha m	Taittiriya Upanishad - II	**SevA:** GopikAstree Raining their hands and making SaraNAgati to Bramha m-Kannan to give back their dresses. Essence of NyAsa VidyA is to surrender completely to Bramha m, and enter-into His Kainkaryam (SevA- serve Him in all possible ways) न्यास इत्याहुर्मनीषिणो ब्रह्माणं ब्रह्मा विश्वः कतमः स्वयम्भुः प्राजपतिः संवत्सर इति । This Vidya says, NyAsa, the surrender to Bramha m is the highest form of everything one could do. To leave surrender, and submit to Him all our responsibilities and burden (भार) is NyAsa.
32	Pratardhana VidyA	Meditation as taught to Pratardana by the god Indra to meditate on Bramha n as AntayAmi (soul) of IndrA.	Kaushitaki Upanishad, III	**PrANA** as ParamatmA Himself. Kaushitaki Upanishad declares that PrANA is life and immortality and one's life span depends on it. Therefore, through meditating PrANA one attains immortality. The Upanishad says selves are supported and held by PrANA. PrANA is Atman, and therefore one should meditate on it. In the VedAnta Sutra 1.1.24 is described as very cause of origination and destruction of all things in the Universe and hence connotes the Bramha m Himself. Between senses and PrANA there was a competition as to who is supreme? It is seen that one of the IndriyAs stopped working, others continued to function, while when PrANA left all other senses departed from the ShreerA.

10. How do we Liberate ourselves from the cycle of birth and death?

While doing ones' Swadharma (Karma,) with **Kartrutva, Mamata and Phala Thyaga,** (As stated by Lord Krishna in many slokas in Bagavat GitA) and simultaneously strive for Liberation (Relief from Samsara-End of Cycle of birth and death). There is huge volume of Literature available in Sanatana Dharma, which we must understand by learning from a Guru, and reading those books published by various authors through many publishing houses, and other specialists on VedAntA field of study. Therefore, **this understanding of Self, and Bramha n, their Lakshanams, (GuNA-Attributes) and relation between them, through a Guru, and carrying out Upasana, of that Bramha m with His Kalyana Gunas, is the essence of any Bramha VidyA.**

It is stated in Upanishads and Veda Poorvangam i.e., Poorva Mimasa (Karma Kandam,) that through this Manushya Shareeram only, one could attain this knowledge, since Buddhi is given to Manushya Janma only. With the help of Buddhi, one understands the Dos and Donts of Shruti, (ShastrA) and Smruti (Itihasa, Purana etc.,) and knows the purpose of this Manushya Janma is **only** to liberate one-self from the Cycle of Birth and Death. As one progresses in learning he also has to **service to the Society, as stipulated in Subhashitani** (Collection of many advises given by Rishis) and Meditation on Bramha n.

परोपकारायफलन्ति वृक्षाः परोपकाराय वहन्तिनद्यः ।

परोपकाराय दुहन्ति गावः परोपकारार्थमिदं शरीरम् ॥

parōpakārāyaphalanti vṛkṣāḥ parōpakārāya vahantinadyaḥ /

parōpakārāya duhanti gāvah parōpakārārthamidaṁ śarīram //

Trees give fruits for others, rivers flow for others, Cows give Milk for others. Likewise, this human body (ShareerA) of ours is for the service of others. Just as Trees will not eat fruits itself, rivers will not drink water herself, cows will not drink milk herself, our body is also for the service of others and not just for ourselves.

Out of the famous "Trio, of Vedanta namely Upanishads, Bramha Sutra, and Bhagavat Gita, first two shows us clearly thirty-two such Bramha VidyAs, leading us to the supreme Bramha m. Some of them, show us the ways to attain worldly benefits or goods also. **These thirty-two VidyAs show us the path of Upasana, (Meditation), and worship with utmost faith.**

"NyAsa-VidyA" is proclaimed as the excellent one by Itihasas, Puranas, and Agamas. Nyasa is called by various names, viz Prapatti, Bharanyasa, Nikshepa, and Sharanagati. According to this VidyA complete surrender to Bramha m, with full faith and conviction, to serve Him eternally and that believe in His capability to give Liberation and save us from all calamities and Mrutyu. (Rakshakatvam). It demands a life, in full agreement with Shastra, and carrying out one's Swadharma, with three thyaga referred above, promising liberation at the end of one's life time itself (or as wished and prayed by a Jiva).

11. Gayatri examples of Bramha Vidya from Upanishads

Gayatri Vidya: (Chandokya Upanishad- 3-12-1)

पूर्णमप्रवर्तनीं श्रियं लभते य एवं वेद

pūrṇāmapravartanīṁ śriyaṁ labhatē ya ēvaṁ vēda

Gayatri VidyA says, that if one equates Bramha m and Gayatri Mantram equally and does Brahmopasanam, he attains wealth which does not leave him.

Gayatri VidyA also says:

गायत्री वा इदं सर्वं भूतं यदिदं किंच। वाग्वै गायत्री। वाग्वा इदं सर्वं भूतं गायति च त्रायते च ॥

gāyatrī vā idaṁ sarvaṁ bhūtaṁ yadidaṁ kiṁca. vāgvai gāyatrī. vāgvā idaṁ sarvaṁ bhūtaṁ gāyati ca trāyatē ca

Whatever we see around is Gayatree only, that itself is Vakku, (speech), that sings, and the same is protecting us. Gayatri is Bramha n Himself.

12. Bramha VidyA rules in Bramha Sutram: (साधन-उपासन-अध्यायम्-|||)

||| गुण उपसंहार पादम्:

1) In all the thirty- two VidyAs the Vidhi, one who is to be taken into DhyAnam, Name of the deity, Roopam etc are all united meaning same and so, they are all ONE VidyA only.

2) Only if Roopam changes, VidyA will change.

3) In Kausheetaki and Chandokya VidyA, PrANa Vidya is same.

4) AnanDAdhi, Swaroopa, Niroopaka DharmAs are to be followed in all VidyAs.

5) Acamana water before and after Bojanam (Eating) is to be treated as Vastram (dress) for PrANA.

6) ShAndilya VidyA stated in both places are same.

7) Aditya mandalam and eyes, (in both these places,) Bramha m's swaroopam is different even though PrANa shareerA and so, to be done UpAsanam separately or differently.

8) AkAsha VyApti also, is to be followed in all places except where they are projected as alpapradesam.

9) Because of Roopa Bedam, what is stated in Taitreeya and Chandokya Upanishads are different.

10) SamnO mitra: etc., are not VidyAs. They are AngA for Upanishads

11) One who leaves for Moksha, leaves behind him his PunyA to friends and Papa to Enemys is to be understood.

12) Before a Mumukshu and UpAsakan, leaves for ArchirAdi mArgA, all his PunyA and PavA must be got rid of.

13) All UPAsaakAs travel through ArchirAdi MArgA only.

14) Nir doshA and, kalyANa GuNA are applicable to all VidyAs.

15) Ushashti Kaholar's question asks many questions. But the answer is one only.i.e., SarvantarAtmA is the deity to be done UpAsanam.

16) vajasaneyagam and Chandokya Dahara VidyAs are same.

17) UdgitopAsana is not YagjnA Angam for Dahara Vidya's.

18) Dahara UpAsanam is to be done with GuNAshtakam, and satyavAdi Swaroopam.

19) NArAyaNAnuvakam establishes that what is seen in other VidyAs, the deity Indru, SivA etc SabdhAs only point to NarAyaNA.

20) Vag-chit and Manas-chit are told, to get VidyAmayakratu siddhi only

21) In ParavIdyA, Bramha m is to be prayed with Special attribute of Bramha m-namely JivAtmA Apahata-PApma

22) Udgita UpAsanA is applicable to all VidyAs.

23) In VaisvAnara VidyA, all AvayavAs are to be included while doing UpAsanA.

24) GuNA and Vidhi where different VidyAs are different.

25) PhalA for all VidyAs are one only and so, it is enough to carry out one VidyA only.

1. *Karmas are angam of UpAsanam and not otherwise.*
2. *Udgita UpAsanam is to be done with Rasatamam*
3. *Swataketu's UpAkyAnAdis are for stotra of each VidyA and not stories.*
4. *Sanyasis are AdhikAris for UpAsanA with their DharmAs.*
5. *VidyAs are to follow YagjnAdi KarmAs.*
6. *Those who do YagjnA also must have Sama, Dama attributes.*
7. *If in emergency (when death like situation arise) UpAsakA can take any food.*
8. *AngAs for uPAsanA, like YagjnA are applicable to Asrama dharmA also. Widowers are also eligible for DhAna, Japa UpAsanams.*
9. *Those who do not follow Ashrama dharmA are not eligible for UpAsanA.*
10. *Udgita etc., which are angams of Vidya are to be carried out by Ruthviks (those who have done VedadyAnam)*
11. *It is very essential for UpAsakAs, to have cintana of Divya Mangala Vigraham.*
12. *UpAsakan should not speak about his prides to others.*
13. *BrahmopAsanam, if not hindered by popular karma, gives immediate PhalA.*
14. *BrahmopAsanam for Mukti might not give immediate PhalA.*
15. *UpAsam is to be done entire life quite often.*
16. *UpAsakan has to assume Bramha m as his AtmA, while doing UpAsanam.*
17. *Manas etc., very low placed while doing UpAsanam has to be taken as highest Deity.*
18. *Keep Aditya Buddhi in UdgitA.*
19. *UpAsanam to be done while sitting only.*
20. *Once Vidya, starts to give phalan, the earlier PavA will go away and latter ones will not stick.*
21. *PunyA done before and after VidyA will not stick also.*
22. *Karma, not started giving effects will only burn.*
23. *Without expectation of PhalA, Nitya and Naimittika Karmas to be carried out compulsorily.*
24. *PrArabda Karma, need not vanish in One birth and one ShareerA*

13. Exhibit-1 - Bramha Vidyopanishad

॥ ब्रह्मविद्योपनिषत् ॥

॥ BRAMHA VIDYOPANIṢAT ॥

स्वाविद्यातत्कार्यजातं यद्विद्यापह्नवं गतम् ।
तद्धंसविद्यानिष्पन्नं रामचन्द्रपदं भजे ॥

svāvidyātatkāryajātaṃ yadvidyāpahnavaṃ gatam ।
taddhaṃsavidyāniṣpannaṃ rāmacandrapadaṃ bhaje ॥

ॐ सह नाववतु ॥ सह नौ भुनक्तु ॥
oṃ saha nāvavatu ॥ saha nau bhunaktu ॥

सह वीर्यं करवावहै ॥
saha vīryaṃ karavavahai ॥

तेजस्विनावधीतमस्तु मा विद्विषावहै ॥
tejasvināvadhītamastu mā vidviṣāvahai ॥

ॐ शान्तिः शान्तिः शान्तिः ॥
oṃ śāntiḥ śāntiḥ śāntiḥ ॥

अथ ब्रह्मविद्योपनिषदुच्यते ॥
atha Bramha vidyopaniṣaducyate ॥

प्रसादाद्ब्रह्मणस्तस्य विष्णोरद्भुतकर्मणः ।
रहस्यं ब्रह्मविद्याया ध्रुवाग्निं सम्प्रचक्षते ॥ १॥

prasādādBramha ṇastasya viṣṇoradbhutakarmaṇaḥ ।
rahasyaṃ Bramha vidyāyā dhruvāgniṃ sampracakṣate ॥ 1 ॥

ॐइत्येकाक्षरं ब्रह्म यदुक्तं ब्रह्मवादिभिः ।
शरीरं तस्य वक्ष्यामि स्थानं कालत्रयं तथा ॥ २॥

omityekākṣaraṃ Bramha yaduktaṃ Bramha vādibhiḥ ।
śarīraṃ tasya vakṣyāmi sthānaṃ kālatrayaṃ tathā ॥ 2 ॥

तत्र देवास्त्रयः प्रोक्ता लोका वेदास्त्रयोऽग्नयः ।
तिस्रो मात्रार्धमात्रा च त्र्यक्षरस्य शिवस्य तु ॥ ३ ॥

tatra devāstrayaḥ proktā lokā vedāstrayo'gnayaḥ ।
tisro mātrārdhamātrā ca tryakṣarasya śivasya tu ॥ 3 ॥

SLOKA 1-3

The indication of the Bramha n, by the PranavA, which contains the

secret significance of Bramha VidyA.

After one has acquired the requisite attainmnets to know Bramha VidyA, he is initiated into Bramha Vidyopanishad for his benefit. By the grace of Bramha n (Vishnu), the steady fire, which reduces to ashes the ignorance, the truth underlying Bramha VidyA is, the Bramha n. It is stated here the monosyllable "Om" is the Bramha n. Now we will relate, what is it's Body, it's seat and three durations. They are three DevAs, three worlds, the three VedAs, three fires, and the three Matras and the half Matra (syllable) of the three lettered ShivA.

ऋग्वेदो गार्हपत्यं च पृथिवी ब्रह्म एव च ।
आकारस्य शरीरं तु व्याख्यातं ब्रह्मवादिभिः ॥ ४॥

ṛgvedo gārhapatyaṃ ca pṛthivī Bramha eva ca |
ākārasya śarīraṃ tu vyākhyātaṃ Bramha vādibhiḥ ॥ 4॥

यजुर्वेदोऽन्तरिक्षं च दक्षिणाग्निस्तथैव च ।
विष्णुश्च भगवान्देव उकारः परिकीर्तितः ॥ ५॥

yajurvedo'ntarikṣaṃ ca dakṣiṇāgnistathaiva ca |
viṣṇuśca bhagavāndeva ukāraḥ parikīrtitaḥ ॥ 5॥

सामवेदस्तथा द्यौश्चाहवनीयस्तथैव च ।
ईश्वरः परमो देवो मकारः परिकीर्तितः ॥ ६॥

sāmavedastathā dyauścāhavanīyastathaiva ca |
īśvaraḥ paramo devo makāraḥ parikīrtitaḥ ॥ 6॥

सूर्यमण्डलमध्येऽथ ह्यकारः शङ्खमध्यगः ।
उकारश्चन्द्रसंकाशस्तस्य मध्ये व्यवस्थितः ॥ ७॥

sūryamaṇḍalamadhye'tha hyakāraḥ śaṅkhamadhyagaḥ |
ukāraścandrasaṃkāśastasya madhye vyavasthitaḥ ॥ 7॥

मकारस्त्वग्निसंकाशो विधूमो विद्युतोपमः ।
तिस्रो मात्रास्तथा ज्ञेया सोमसूर्याग्निरूपिणः ॥ ८॥

makārastvagnisaṃkāśo vidhūmo vidyutopamaḥ |
tisro mātrāstathā jñeyā somasūryāgnirūpiṇaḥ ॥ 8॥

शिखा तु दीपसंकाशा तस्मिन्नुपरि वर्तते ।
अर्धमात्र तथा ज्ञेया प्रणवस्योपरि स्थिता ॥ ९॥

śikhā tu dīpasaṃkāśā tasminnupari vartate |
ardhamātra tathā jñeyā praṇavasyopari sthitā || 9 ||

SLOKA 4-9/PraNava Charateristics

The body of the **"अ-A"**, of the Pranava, as stated in RgvedA, the Garhapatya
fire, the earth and God Bramha n.

The **"उ-U"** of the Pranava, as stated in Yajurveda, Antariksha (the middle
world), Dakshina Fire and Lord Vishnu.

The **"म्-M"** of the Pranava, as stated in Samaveda, and Swarga loka (upper
region), the Ahavaniya fire, and Para Bramha n IswarA.

The three Matra syllable are similarly to be understood, as one of the forms of
the Moon, Sun, and the Fire. Even as the flame of the lam stands over it, so
also should the ArdhamAtrA to be understood, as   standing over the Pranava

पद्मसूत्रनिभा सूक्ष्मा शिखा सा दृश्यते परा ।
सा नाडी सूर्यसंकाशा सूर्यं भित्त्वा तथापरा ॥ १०॥

padmasūtranibhā sūkṣmā śikhā sā dṛśyate parā |
sā nāḍī sūryasaṃkāśā sūryam bhittvā tathāparā || 10 ||

द्विसप्ततिसहस्राणि नाडीं भित्वा च मूर्धनि ।
वरदः सर्वभूतानां सर्वं व्याप्यावतिष्ठति ॥ ११॥

dvisaptatisahasrāṇi nāḍīṃ bhittvā ca mūrdhani |
varadaḥ sarvabhūtānāṃ sarvaṃ vyāpyāvatiṣṭhati ॥ 11॥

The transcendent (Sushumna) flame is seen to be as subtle as the fibre of the Lotus-stalk. The transcendent Nadi, resembling the Sun and bursting through the Sun and similarly bursting as under the 72000 Nadis, pervading all, stands in the head as if he is giver of the boons to all beings.

कांस्यघण्टानिनादस्तु यथा लीयति शान्तये ।
ओङ्कारस्तु तथा योज्यः शान्तये सर्वमिच्छता ॥ १२॥

kāṃsyaghaṇṭāninādastu yathā līyati śāntaye |
oṅkārastu tathā yojyaḥ śāntaye sarvamicchatā ॥ 12॥

यस्मिन्विलीयते शब्दस्तत्परं ब्रह्म गीयते ।
धियं हि लीयते ब्रह्म सोऽमृतत्वाय कल्पते ॥ १३॥

yasminvilīyate śabdastatparaṃ Bramha gīyate |
dhiyaṃ hi līyate Bramha so'mṛtatvāya kalpate ॥ 13॥

*Attainment of liberation by the Laya aur or dissolution
of the of the sound of the Pranava*

That Yogin who dissolves his inner sense (that is Manas-the Mind) along with the sound of PranavA of sixteen MAtrAs, attains oneness with Bramha n, giving up the delusion of existence apart from the Atman. (This is Advaitic concept). Atma-SamarpaNam is done with PraNavA alone according to ShAstrA.

वायुः प्राणस्तथाकाशस्त्रिविधो जीवसंज्ञकः ।
स जीवः प्राण इत्युक्तो वालाग्रशतकल्पितः ॥ १४॥

vāyuḥ prāṇastathākāśastrividho jīvasaṃjñakaḥ ।
sa jīvaḥ prāṇa ityukto vālāgraśatakalpitaḥ ॥ 14॥

नाभिस्थाने स्थितं विश्वं शुद्धतत्त्वं सुनिर्मलम् ।
आदित्यमिव दीप्यन्तं रश्मिभिश्चाखिलं शिवम् ॥ १५॥

nābhisthāne sthitaṃ viśvaṃ śuddhatattvaṃ sunirmalam ।
ādityamiva dīpyantaṃ raśmibhiścākhilaṃ śivam ॥ 15॥

SLOKA 14-15 Exposition of the real form of the Jiva

That which is Called the JivA, is Vital air (PrAnA), radiance and the ether. The JivA is known as PrANA which is made of one-hundredth part of the awn of a grain of wild paddy.

सकारं च हकारं च जीवो जपति सर्वदा ।
नाभिरन्ध्राद्विनिष्क्रान्तं विषयव्याप्तिविवर्जितम् ॥ १६॥

sakāraṃ ca hakāraṃ ca jīvo japati sarvadā |
nābhirandhrādviniṣkrāntaṃ viṣayavyāptivarjitam ॥ 16॥

तेनेदं निष्कलं विद्यात्क्षीरात्सर्पिर्यथा तथा ।
कारणेनात्मना युक्तः प्राणायामैश्च पञ्चभिः ॥ १७॥

tenedaṃ niṣkalaṃ vidyātkṣīrātsarpiryathā tathā |
kāraṇenātmanā yuktaḥ prāṇāyāmaiśca pañcabhiḥ ॥ 17॥

चतुष्कला समायुक्तो भ्राम्यते च हृदिस्थितः ।
गोलकस्तु यदा देहे क्षीरदण्डेन वा हतः ॥ १८॥

catuṣkalā samāyukto bhrāmyate ca hṛdisthitaḥ |
golakastu yadā dehe kṣīradaṇḍena vā hataḥ ॥ 18॥

एतस्मिन्वसते शीघ्रमविश्रान्तं महाखगः ।
यावन्निश्वसितो जीवस्तावन्निष्कलतां गतः ॥ १९॥

etasminvasate śīghramaviśrāntaṃ mahākhagaḥ |
yāvanniśvasito jīvastāvanniṣkalatāṃ gataḥ ॥ 19॥

नभस्थं निष्कलं ध्यात्वा मुच्यते भवबन्धनात्
अनाहतध्वनियुतं हंसं यो वेद हृद्गतम् ॥ २०॥

nabhasthaṃ niṣkalaṃ dhyātvā mucyate bhavabandhanāt
anāhatadhvaniyutaṃ haṃsaṃ yo veda hṛdgatam ॥ 20॥

Exposition of the cause of bondage and liberation

The JivA always recites the PraNavA with "I" and "He" consciousness. One should know this that "type of breadth going in and out, emanates from the region of navel is uncontaminated by connection with worldly concerns". JivA becomes one with Bramha n, through five-fold PrANAyAmA (i.e., PrANAyAmA, PratyAhArA, DhAraNa, DhyANA and SamAdhi) and engages itself in the heart with four-fold aspects of Vishva, Taijasa, PragnjA, and Turiya, and engages itself in the investigation of bondage, liberation, and their effects. As long as, Atman does not attain the knowledge, it restlessly wanders in and out, and once Atma Gjana is attained, the outgoing breadth carries with it, (JivA's internal organ stops functioning) the JivA attain state of cessation of diverse aspects and attains liberation by meditating upon the Bramha n in the heart of PratygAtmA. (one's self Atma)

स्वप्रकाशचिदानन्दं स हंस इति गीयते ।
रेचकं पूरकं मुक्त्वा कुम्भकेन स्थितः सुधीः ॥ २१॥

svaprakāśacidānandaṃ sa haṃsa iti gīyate |
recakaṃ pūrakaṃ muktvā kumbhakena sthitaḥ sudhīḥ ॥ 21 ॥

नाभिकन्दे समौ कृत्वा प्राणापानौ समाहितः ।
मस्तकस्थामृतास्वादं पीत्वा ध्यानेन सादरम् ॥ २२॥

nābhikande samau kṛtvā prāṇāpānau samāhitaḥ |
mastakasthāmṛtāsvādaṃ pītvā dhyānena sādaram ॥ 22 ॥

दीपाकारं महादेवं ज्वलन्तं नाभिमध्यमे ।
अभिषिच्यामृतेनैव हंस हंसेति यो जपेत् ॥ २३॥

dīpākāraṃ mahādevaṃ jvalantaṃ nābhimadhyame |
abhiṣicyāmṛtenaiva haṃsa haṃseti yo japet ॥ 23 ॥

जरामरणरोगादि न तस्य भुवि विद्यते ।

एवं दिने दिने कुर्यादणिमादिविभूतये ॥ २४॥

jarāmaraṇarogādi na tasya bhuvi vidyate |

evaṃ dine dine kuryādaṇimādivibhūtaye ॥ 24॥

ईश्वरत्वमवाप्नोति सदाभ्यासरतः पुमान् ।

बहवो नैकमार्गेण प्राप्ता नित्यत्वमागताः ॥ २५॥

īśvaratvamavāpnoti sadābhyāsarataḥ pumān |

bahavo naikamārgeṇa prāptā nityatvamāgatāḥ ॥ 25॥

---

*Exposition of the cause of bondage and liberation
through hamsa vidya*

A yogi should after giving up Recaka, and Puraka must concentrate on Kumbaka, and bring PrANA and ApAnA vayus under equilibrium. Then "Hamsa" recitation brings him no death or disease in the world. All the side effects of getting siddhis on the way should never be misused. Then One attains oneness with Bramha n. (Wielding marvellous Yogic Power) If Hamsa Vidya stops there is no means for attaining state of perpetual existence. Hamsa Vidya is the fifteenth among 108 Upanishads, and forms part of Sukla Yajur Veda. This also deals with esoteric nature of the Hamsavidya leading to Bramha Vidya.

This is formed in the manner of Question by Gautama Muni to Santkumara:

Gautama asks, "By what means is produced the awakening in the lore of Bramha n?

Sanatkumara answers:

Hamsa Vidya is explained here by Sanatkumara; but he cautions that one has to learn it through a Guru and should not be communicated to those who do not believe in Bramha m. The detailed elaboration of the aspect of the Hamsa, bestows the fruit resulting from liberation. This denies enjoyment of everything except the Atma. The state of aloneness.

Hamsa Vidya Concept: Hamsa stands pervading the bodies of all beings from PrajApati the catur mukha Bramha down to a blade of grass, in the form of innermost JivA, and the transcendent Bramha n-IshwarA) Having known that form, the knower does not attain the delusion relating to the existence of anything except Bramha n. Yoga clearly explains the way to attain the knowledge of Hamsa.

Explanation of Hamsa MantrA (Author's note)

Hamsa is the rsi. (The seer of the mantra) Avyakta gayatri is the Chandas, Paramahamsa (Bramha n is the deity) Ham is the Bija (Seed) Sah is the power(shakti) Soham is the Kilaka. In having the direct sight of the Hamsatman is the application (Viniyoga) Ham-sam is the Sixfold Anganyasa.

Now -Meditation (DhyAnA): I make salutations to the Hamsa i.e., who is the form of ParamAtmA, on whom the seekers and knowers of Bramha n, meditate who takes his stand of the incoming and outgoing breadth, and with many other KalyANa GuNAs, takes His stand on the midst of mortals. Then the worship of the five elements, with their Bija letters Lam etc., So, Ham (I am He) is the Mantra. Exhale, inhale and reversal of the same alone constitute the Prayer. The uttering of the Prayer, as computed at the six centres of energy (by the presiding deities thereof) in the course of one day and night is 21600 times (in the form of So-Ham through expiration and inspiration) it goes on to explain the details which could be well read in YogA texts.

हंसविद्यामृते लोके नास्ति नित्यत्वसाधनम् ।
यो ददाति महाविद्यां हंसाख्यां पारमेश्वरीम् ॥ २६॥

haṃsavidyāmṛte loke nāsti nityatvasādhanam ।
yo dadāti mahāvidyāṃ haṃsākhyāṃ parameśvarīm ॥ 26॥

तस्य दास्यं सदा कुर्यात्प्रज्ञया परया सह ।
शुभं वाऽशुभमन्यद्वा यदुक्तं गुरुणा भुवि ॥ २७॥

tasya dāsyaṃ sadā kuryātprajñayā parayā saha ।
śubhaṃ vā'śubhamanyadvā yaduktaṃ guruṇā bhuvi ॥ 27॥

तत्कुर्यादविचारेण शिष्यः सन्तोषसंयुतः ।
हंसविद्यामिमां लब्ध्वा गुरुशुश्रूषया नरः ॥ २८॥

tatkuryādavicāreṇa śiṣyaḥ santoṣasaṃyutaḥ ।
haṃsavidyāmimāṃ labdhvā guruśuśrūṣayā naraḥ ॥ 28॥

आत्मानमात्मना साक्षाद्ब्रह्म बुद्ध्वा सुनिश्चलम् ।
देहजात्यादिसम्बन्धान्वर्णाश्रमसमन्वितान् ॥ २९॥

ātmānamātmanā sākṣādBramha buddhvā suniścalam ।
dehajātyādisambandhānvarṇāśramasamanvitān ॥ 29॥

वेदशास्त्राणि चान्यानि पदपांसुमिव त्यजेत् ।
गुरुभक्तिं सदा कुर्याच्छ्रेयसे भूयसे नरः ॥ ३०॥

vedaśāstrāṇi cānyāni padapāṃsumiva tyajet |
gurubhaktiṃ sadā kuryācchreyase bhūyase naraḥ ॥ 30॥

गुरुरेव हरिः साक्षान्नान्य इत्यब्रवीच्छ्रुतिः ॥ ३१॥

gurureva hariḥ sākṣānnānya ityabravīcchṛtiḥ ॥ 31 ॥

Rule of devotion to the guru of hamsavidya

Sruti states the importance Hamsa Vidya, Guru Thus:

He who wants to know the Highest Hamsa vidya always to service Him, with superior wisdom. Whatever in this world, productive of happiness, misery, or otherwise is the mandate of the Guru, that the disciple should carry out with utmost, pleasure, without any scruple whatsoever. Once this highest knowledge is obtained through the Guru, that Atman is no other than non-fickle Bramha n, that person should renounce the SamsArA along with VAsanAs, and treat Guru with extreme reverence. Guru alone is Hari incarnate says Sruti.

श्रुत्या यदुक्तं परमार्थमेव
तत्संशयो नात्र ततः समस्तम् ।

श्रुत्या विरोधे न भवेत्प्रमाणं
भवेदनर्थाय विना प्रमाणम् ॥ ३२॥

śrutyā yaduktaṃ paramārthameva
tatsaṃśayo nātra tataḥ samastam ।
śrutyā virodhe na bhavetpramāṇaṃ
bhavedanarthāya vinā pramāṇam ॥ 32॥

देहस्थः सकलो ज्ञेयो निष्कलो देहवर्जितः ।
आप्तोपदेशगम्योऽसौ सर्वतः समवस्थितः ॥ ३३॥

dehasthaḥ sakalo jñeyo niṣkalo dehavarjitaḥ ।
āptopadeśagamyo'sau sarvataḥ samavasthitaḥ ॥ 33॥

हंसहंसेति यो ब्रूयाद्धंसो ब्रह्मा हरिः शिवः ।
गुरुवक्त्रात्तु लभ्येत प्रत्यक्षं सर्वतोमुखम् ॥ ३४॥

haṃsahaṃseti yo brūyāddhaṃso brahmā hariḥ śivaḥ ।
guruvaktrāttu labhyeta pratyakṣaṃ sarvatomukham ॥ 34॥

तिलेषु च यथा तैलं पुष्पे गन्ध इवाश्रितः ।
पुरुषस्य शरीरेऽस्मिन्स बाह्याभ्यन्तरे तथा ॥ ३५॥

tileṣu ca yathā tailaṃ puṣpe gandha ivāśritaḥ ।
puruṣasya śarīre'sminsa bāhyābhyantare tathā ॥ 35॥

*The attainability of the Bramha n solelythrough vedas
and guru*

He (Bramha n) stands, pervading the exterior and interior of all beings that is created. And one should obtain this secret through the mouth of an experienced Guru. What is related by VedA is the supreme end of the existence. There is no doubt about it. Therefrom flow all things. Should there be divergence from VedA that will not afford sanction. Anything without sanction will contribute towards utter ruin Bramha n is attainable only through sound precept. Why then Bramha n is said to be in all direction. Those who have had MantrOpadesam through a Guru, is directly cognisized, and faces in all directions.

उल्काहस्तो यथालोके द्रव्यमालोक्य तां त्यजेत् ।
ज्ञानेन ज्ञेयमालोक्य पश्चाज्ज्ञानं परित्यजेत् ॥ ३६॥

ulkāhasto yathāloke dravyamālokya tāṃ tyajet ।
jñānena jñeyamālokya paścājjñānaṃ parityajet ॥ 36॥

पुष्पवत्सकलं विद्याद्गन्धस्तस्य तु निष्कलः ।
वृक्षस्तु सकलं विद्याच्छाया तस्य तु निष्कला ॥ ३७॥

puṣpavatsakalaṃ vidyādgandhastasya tu niṣkalaḥ ।
vṛkṣastu sakalaṃ vidyācchāyā tasya tu niṣkalā ॥ 37॥

निष्कलः सकलो भावः सर्वत्रैव व्यवस्थितः ।
उपायः सकलस्तद्वदुपेयश्चैव निष्कलः ॥ ३८॥

niṣkalaḥ sakalo bhāvaḥ sarvatraiva vyavasthitaḥ |
upāyaḥ sakalastadvadupeyaścaiva niṣkalaḥ ॥ 38॥

सकले सकलो भावो निष्कले निष्कलस्तथा ।
एकमात्रो द्विमात्रश्च त्रिमात्रश्चैव भेदतः ॥ ३९॥

sakale sakalo bhāvo niṣkale niṣkalastathā |
ekamātro dvimātraśca trimātraścaiva bhedataḥ ॥ 39॥

अर्धमात्र परा ज्ञेया तत ऊर्ध्वं परात्परम् ।
पञ्चधा पञ्चदैवत्यं सकलं परिपठ्यते ॥ ४०॥

ardhamātra parā jñeyā tata ūrdhvaṃ parātparam |
pañcadhā pañcadaivatyam sakalam paripaṭhyate ॥ 40॥

ब्रह्मणो हृदयस्थानं कण्ठे विष्णुः समाश्रितः ।
तालुमध्ये स्थितो रुद्रो ललाटस्थो महेश्वरः ॥ ४१॥

Bramha no hṛdayasthānam kaṇṭhe viṣṇuḥ samāśritaḥ |
tālumadhye sthito rudro lalāṭastho maheśvaraḥ ॥ 41॥

नासाग्रे अच्युतं विद्यात्तस्यान्ते तु परं पदम् ।
परत्वात्तु परं नास्तीत्येवं शास्त्रस्य निर्णयः ॥ ४२॥

nāsāgre acyutaṃ vidyāttasyānte tu param padam |
paratvāttu param nāstītyevam śāstrasya nirṇayaḥ ॥ 42॥

देहातीतं तु तं विद्यान्नासाग्रे द्वादशाङ्गुलम् ।
तदन्तं तं विजानीयात्तत्रस्थो व्यापयेत्प्रभुः ॥ ४३॥

dehātītaṃ tu taṃ vidyānnāsāgre dvādaśāṅgulam |
tadantaṃ taṃ vijānīyāttatrastho vyāpayetprabhuḥ ॥ 43॥

Discriminating between the finite and the Infinite forms
of the Atman

मनोऽप्यन्यत्र निक्षिप्तं चक्षुरन्यत्र पातितम् ।
तथापि योगिनां योगो ह्यविच्छिन्नः प्रवर्तते ॥ ४४॥

mano'pyanyatra nikṣiptaṃ cakṣuranyatra pātitam |
tathāpi yogināṃ yogo hyavicchinnaḥ pravartate ॥ 44॥

एतत्तु परमं गुह्यमेतत्तु परमं शुभम् ।
नातः परतरं किञ्चिन्नातः परतरं शुभम् ॥ ४५॥

etattu paramaṃ guhyametattu paramaṃ śubham |
nātaḥ parataraṃ kiñcinnātaḥ parataraṃ śubham ॥ 45॥

शुद्धज्ञानामृतं प्राप्य परमाक्षरनिर्णयम् ।
गुह्यादुह्यतमं गोप्यं ग्रहणीयं प्रयत्नतः ॥ ४६॥

śuddhajñānāmṛtaṃ prāpya paramākṣaranirṇayam |
guhyādguhyatamam gopyaṃ grahaṇīyaṃ prayatnataḥ ॥ 46॥

नापुत्राय प्रदातव्यं नाशिष्याय कदाचन ।
गुरुदेवाय भक्ताय नित्यं भक्तिपराय च ॥ ४७॥

nāputrāya pradātavyaṃ nāśiṣyāya kadācana ।
gurudevāya bhaktāya nityaṃ bhaktiparāya ca ॥ 47॥

प्रदातव्यमिदं शास्त्रं नेतरेभ्यः प्रदापयेत् ।
दातास्य नरकं याति सिद्ध्यते न कदाचन ॥ ४८॥

pradātavyamidaṃ śāstraṃ netarebhyaḥ pradāpayet ।
dātāsya narakaṃ yāti siddhyate na kadācana ॥ 48॥

The Yoga to be kept a profound secret from the unqualified, could be bestowed only on those best qualified for it

---

गृहस्थो ब्रह्मचारी च वानप्रस्थश्च भिक्षुकः ।
यत्र तत्र स्थितो ज्ञानी परमाक्षरवित्सदा ॥ ४९॥

gṛhastho Bramha cārī ca vānaprasthaśca bhikṣukaḥ ।
yatra tatra sthito jñānī paramākṣaravitsadā ॥ 49॥

विषयी विषयासक्तो याति देहान्तरे शुभम् ।
ज्ञानादेवास्य शास्त्रस्य सर्वावस्थोऽपि मानवः ॥ ५०॥

viṣayī viṣayāsakto yāti dehāntare śubham |

jñānādevāsya śāstrasya sarvāvastho'pi mānavaḥ || 50||

SLOKA 49-50

This highest knowledge alone does not give someone
vice and virtue

Only by acquiring this knowledge alone through a Guru does not give happiness to someone entering other body.

ब्रह्महत्याश्वमेधाद्यैः पुण्यपापैर्न लिप्यते ।

चोदको बोधकश्चैव मोक्षदश्च परः स्मृतः ॥ ५१॥

Bramha hatyāśvamedhādyaiḥ puṇyapāpairna lipyate |

codako bodhakaścaiva mokṣadaśca paraḥ smṛtaḥ || 51 ||

इत्येषं त्रिविधो ज्ञेय आचार्यस्तु महीतले ।

चोदको दर्शयेन्मार्गं बोधकः स्थानमाचरेत् ॥ ५२॥

ityeṣaṃ trividho jñeya ācāryastu mahītale |

codako darśayenmārgaṃ bodhakaḥ sthānamācaret || 52||

SLOKA 51-52

Who is real perceptor (three things he must do)

Supreme Guru should do following to his ShishyA.

The prompter, the awakener, and the bestower of Liberation

मोक्षदस्तु परं तत्त्वं यज्ज्ञात्वा परमश्रुते ।
प्रत्यक्षयजनं देहे संक्षेपाच्छृणु गौतम ॥ ५३॥

mokṣadastu param tattvam yajjñātvā paramaśnute |
pratyakṣayajanam dehe samkṣepācchṛṇu gautama ॥ 53॥

तेनेष्ट्वा स नरो याति शाश्वतं पदमव्ययम् ।
स्वयमेव तु सम्पश्येद्देहे बिन्दुं च निष्कलम् ॥ ५४॥

teneṣṭvā sa naro yāti śāśvatam padamavyayam |
svayameva tu sampaśyeddehe bindum ca niṣkalam ॥ 54॥

अयने द्वे च विषुवे सदा पश्यति मार्गवित् ।
कृत्वायामं पुरा वत्स रेचपूरककुम्भकान् ॥ ५५॥

ayane dve ca viṣuve sadā paśyati mārgavit |
kṛtvāyāmam purā vatsa recapūrakakumbhakān ॥ 55॥

पूर्वं चोभयमुच्चार्य अर्चयेतु यथाक्रमम् ।
नमस्कारेण योगेन मुद्रयारभ्य चार्चयेत् ॥ ५६॥

pūrvam cobhayamuccārya arcayettu yathākramam |
namaskāreṇa yogena mudrayārabhya cārcayet ॥ 56॥

*The performance of sacrifice in the immediate presence
of Bramhan by applying pranava hamsa*

Briefly, the sacrifice to be performed in the immediate presence of Bramha n, is in the Body itself. Whence performed this, the sacrifice reaches the eternal and undecaying state. This sacrifice is performed thus:

Perform Recaka, Puraka and Kumbaka for one Yama (three hours) every day, and then if recited the Japa, the PraNavA and Hamsa MantrA, along with application of his mind to their fullest in the proper order and reverently worship the Bramha n, commencing with prostration and assuming with Chin MudrA and uttering the word He am I, being lost in communion with it. The eclipse of the Sun is thought of as direct sacrifice.

सूर्यस्य ग्रहणं वत्स प्रत्यक्षयजनं स्मृतम् ।
ज्ञानात्सायुज्यमेवोक्तं तोये तोयं यथा तथा ॥ ५७॥

sūryasya grahaṇaṃ vatsa pratyakṣayajanaṃ smṛtam |
jñānātsāyujyamevoktaṃ toye toyaṃ yathā tathā ॥ 57॥

एते गुणाः प्रवर्तन्ते योगाभ्यासकृतश्रमैः ।
तस्माद्योगं समादाय सर्वदुःखबहिष्कृतः ॥ ५८॥

ete guṇāḥ pravartante yogābhyāsakṛtaśramaiḥ |
tasmādyogaṃ samādāya sarvaduḥkhabahiṣkṛtaḥ ॥ 58॥

योगध्यानं सदा कृत्वा ज्ञानं तन्मयतां व्रजेत् ।
ज्ञानात्स्वरूपं परमं हंसमन्त्रं समुच्चरेत् ॥ ५९॥

yogadhyānaṃ sadā kṛtvā jñānaṃ tanmayatāṃ vrajet |
jñānātsvarūpaṃ paramaṃ haṃsamantraṃ samuccaret || 59||

The attainment of becoming one with the Bramha n
through the knowledge obtained from hamsa yoga

It has been said that from knowledge is attained, oneness of Atman and
Bramha n. For this practice, the Yogin become s one with Bramha n, and the
Yogin is divorced from all sufferings, and pain. Therefore, one should always
practice Yogic Meditation and attain wisdom, and with this wisdom merge
with Bramha n.

प्राणिनां देहमध्ये तु स्थितो हंसः सदाच्युतः ।
हंस एव परं सत्यं हंस एव तु शक्तिकम् ॥ ६०॥

prāṇināṃ dehamadhye tu sthito haṃsaḥ sadācyutaḥ |
haṃsa eva paraṃ satyaṃ haṃsa eva tu śaktikam || 60||

हंस एव परं वाक्यं हंस एव तु वादिकम् ।
हंस एव परो रुद्रो हंस एव परात्परम् ॥ ६१॥

haṃsa eva paraṃ vākyaṃ haṃsa eva tu vādikam |
haṃsa eva paro rudro haṃsa eva parātparam || 61||

सर्वदेवस्य मध्यस्थो हंस एव महेश्वरः ।
पृथिव्यादिशिवान्तं तु अकाराद्याश्च वर्णकाः ॥ ६२॥

sarvadevasya madhyastho haṃsa eva maheśvaraḥ ।
pṛthivyādiśivāntaṃ tu akārādyāśca varṇakāḥ ॥ 62॥

The place for acquiring hamsa

Hamsa the Bramha n has His abode in the Heart in the middle of the body of all beings along with all His KalyaNa guNA. He alone is attached to fifty-one letters (AksharA) commencing from **"अ"** and ending with Koota" (Ksha) **"क्ष"**

कूटान्ता हंस एव स्यान्मातृकेति व्यवस्थिताः ।
मातृकारहितं मन्त्रमादिशन्ते न कुत्रचित् ॥ ६३॥

kūṭāntā haṃsa eva syānmātṛketi vyavasthitāḥ ।
mātṛkārahitaṃ mantramādiśante na kutracit ॥ 63॥

हंसज्योतिरनूपम्यं मध्ये देवं व्यवस्थितम् ।
दक्षिणामुखमाश्रित्य ज्ञानमुद्रां प्रकल्पयेत् ॥ ६४॥

haṃsajyotiranūpamyaṃ madhye devaṃ vyavasthitam ।
dakṣiṇāmukhamāśritya jñānamudrāṃ prakalpayet ॥ 64॥

सदा समाधिं कुर्वीत हंसमन्त्रमनुस्मरन् ।
निर्मलस्फटिकाकारं दिव्यरूपमनुत्तमम् ॥ ६५॥

sadā samādhiṃ kurvīta haṃsamantramanusmaran |
nirmalasphaṭikākāraṃ divyarūpamanuttamam || 65||

Nowhere, do people recognise a Mantra made up of sounds which have no counterparts in the alphabet. One should seek protection at the hands of the Hamsa radiance well placed with GjAna MudrA (ज्ञानमुद्रा) posture. He should be always be concentrated and always reciting the Hamsa -mantra.

मध्यदेशे परं हंसं ज्ञानमुद्रात्मरूपकम् ।
प्राणोऽपानः समानश्चोदानव्यानौ च वायवः || ६६||

madhyadeśe param haṃsam jñānamudrātmarūpakam |
prāṇo'pānah samānaścodānavyānau ca vāyavaḥ || 66||

पञ्चकर्मेन्द्रियैरुक्ताः क्रियाशक्तिबलोद्यताः ।
नागः कूर्मश्च कृकरो देवदत्तो धनञ्जयः || ६७||

pañcakarmendriyairuktāḥ kriyāśaktibalodyatāḥ |
nāgaḥ kūrmaśca kṛkaro devadatto dhanañjayaḥ || 67||

पञ्चज्ञानेन्द्रियैर्युक्ता ज्ञानशक्तिबलोद्यताः ।
पावकः शक्तिमध्ये तु नाभिचक्रे रविः स्थितः || ६८||

pañcajñānendriyairyuktā jñānaśaktibalodyatāḥ |
pāvakaḥ śaktimadhye tu nābhicakre raviḥ sthitaḥ || 68||

Exposition of posture assumed by hamsa

Pure Yogic explanation:

The five vital airs Prana, Apana, Samana, Udana and Vyana, in conjunction with five inner senses are enthused by the strength of Kriya shakti (Power of doing deeds) the five vital airs, Naga, Kurma, krkara, Devadatta, and Dhananjaya in conjunction with inner senses of perception are enthused by the strength of Gjana shakti (the power of knowledge) Hamsa alone stands in the fire midway between two shaktis.

बन्धमुद्रा कृता येन नासाग्रे तु स्वलोचने |
अकारेवह्निरित्याहुरुकारे हृदि संस्थितः || ६९||

bandhamudrā kṛtā yena nāsāgre tu svalocane |
akārevahnirityāhurukāre hṛdi saṃsthitaḥ || 69||

मकारे च भ्रुवोर्मध्ये प्राणशक्त्या प्रबोधयेत् |
ब्रह्मग्रन्थिरकारे च विष्णुग्रन्थिर्हृदि स्थितः || ७०||

makāre ca bhruvormadhye prāṇaśaktyā prabodhayet |
Bramha granthirakāre ca viṣṇugranthirhṛdi sthitaḥ || 70||

रुद्रग्रन्थिर्भ्रुवोर्मध्ये भिद्यतेऽक्षरवायुना ।
अकारे संस्थितो ब्रह्मा उकारे विष्णुरास्थितः ॥ ७१॥

rudragranthirbhruvormadhye bhidyate'kṣaravāyunā ।
akāre saṃsthito brahmā ukāre viṣṇurāsthitaḥ ॥ 71॥

मकारे संस्थितो रुद्रस्ततोऽस्यान्तः परात्परः ।
कण्ठं सङ्कुच्य नाड्यादौ स्तम्भिते येन शक्तितः ॥ ७२॥

makāre saṃsthito rudrastato'syāntaḥ parātparaḥ ।
kaṇṭhaṃ saṅkucya nāḍyādau stambhite yena śaktitaḥ ॥ 72॥

रसना पीड्यमानेयं षोडशी वोर्ध्वगामिनि ।
त्रिकूटं त्रिविधा चैव गोलाखं निखरं तथा ॥ ७३॥

rasanā pīḍyamāneyaṃ ṣoḍaśī vordhvagāmini ।
trikūṭaṃ trividhā caiva golākhaṃ nikharaṃ tathā ॥ 73॥

त्रिशङ्खवज्रमोङ्कारमूर्ध्वनालं भ्रुवोर्मुखम् ।
कुण्डलीं चालयन्प्राणान्भेदयन्शशिमण्डलम् ॥ ७४॥

triśaṅkhavajramoṅkāramūrdhvanālaṃ bhruvormukham ।
kuṇḍalīṃ cālayanprāṇānbhedayanśaśimaṇḍalam ॥ 74॥

साधयन्वज्रकुम्भानि नवद्वाराणि बन्धयेत् ।
सुमनःपवनारूढः सरागो निर्गुणस्तथा ॥ ७५॥

sādhayanvajrakumbhāni navadvārāṇi bandhayet ।
sumanaḥpavanārūḍhaḥ sarāgo nirguṇastathā ॥ 75॥

ब्रह्मस्थाने तु नादः स्याच्छाकिन्यामृतवर्षिणी ।
षट्चक्रमण्डलोद्धारं ज्ञानदीपं प्रकाशयेत् ॥ ७६॥

Bramha sthāne tu nādaḥ syācchākinyāmṛtavarṣiṇī ।
ṣaṭcakramaṇḍaloddhāraṃ jñānadīpaṃ prakāśayet ॥ 76॥

सर्वभूतस्थितं देवं सर्वेशं नित्यमर्चयेत् ।
आत्मरूपं तमालोक्य ज्ञानरूपं निरामयम् ॥ ७७॥

sarvabhūtasthitaṃ devaṃ sarveśaṃ nityamarcayet ।
ātmarūpaṃ tamālokya jñānarūpaṃ nirāmayam ॥ 77॥

दृश्यन्तं दिव्यरूपेण सर्वव्यापी निरञ्जनः ।
हंस हंस वदेद्वाक्यं प्राणिनां देहमाश्रितः ।
सप्राणापानयोर्ग्रन्थिरजपेत्यभिधीयते ॥ ७८॥

dṛśyantaṃ divyarūpeṇa sarvavyāpī nirañjanaḥ ।
haṃsa haṃsa vadedvākyaṃ prāṇināṃ dehamāśritaḥ ।
saprāṇāpānayorgranthirajapetyabhidhīyate ॥ 78॥

सहस्रमेकं द्वयुतं षट्शतं चैव सर्वदा ।
उच्चरन्पठितो हंसः सोऽहमित्यभिधीयते ॥ ७९॥

sahasramekaṃ dvayutaṃ ṣaṭśataṃ caiva sarvadā ।
uccaranpaṭhito haṃsaḥ so'hamityabhidhīyate ॥ 79॥

पूर्वभागे ह्यधोलिङ्गं शिखिन्यां चैव पश्चिमम् ।
ज्योतिर्लिङ्गं भ्रुवोर्मध्ये नित्यं ध्यायेत्सदा यतिः ॥ ८०॥

pūrvabhāge hyadholiṅgaṃ śikhinyāṃ caiva paścimam |

jyotirliṅgaṃ bhruvormadhye nityaṃ dhyāyetsadā yatiḥ || 80||

Utterance of Pranava is what transcends knots in the Nadis and supreme being the Bramha n. Then Kundalini Yoga and moving that shakti up is described. In the seat of Bramha n, there will become manifest the nada. (sound) Knower of Bramha n should then worship Bramha n in the form of knowledge.

अच्युतोऽहमचिन्त्योऽहमतर्क्योऽहमजोऽस्म्यहम् |
अप्राणोऽहमकायोऽहमनङ्गोऽस्म्यभयोऽस्म्यहम् || ८१||

acyuto'hamacintyo'hamatarkyo'hamajo'smyaham |

aprāṇo'hamakāyo'hamanaṅgo'smyabhayo'smyaham || 81||

अशब्दोऽहमरूपोऽहमस्पर्शोऽस्म्यहमद्वयः |
अरसोऽहमगन्धोऽहमनादिरमृतोऽस्म्यहम् || ८२||

aśabdo'hamarūpo'hamasparśo'smyahamadvayaḥ |

araso'hamagandho'hamanādiramṛto'smyaham || 82||

अक्षयोऽहमलिङ्गोऽहमजरोऽस्म्यकलोऽस्म्यहम् |
अप्राणोऽहममूकोऽहमचिन्त्योऽस्म्यकृतोऽस्म्यहम् || ८३||

akṣayo'hamaliṅgo'hamajaro'smyakalo'smyaham |
aprāṇo'hamamūko'hamacintyo'smyakṛto'smyaham || 83 ||

अन्तर्याम्यहमग्राह्योऽनिर्देश्योऽहमलक्षणः |
अगोत्रोऽहमगात्रोऽहमचक्षुष्कोऽस्म्यवागहम् || ८४ ||

antaryāmyahamagrāhyo'nirdeśyo'hamalakṣaṇaḥ |
agotro'hamagātro'hamacakṣuṣko'smyavāgaham || 84 ||

अदृश्योऽहमवर्णोऽहमखण्डोऽस्म्यहमद्भुतः |
अश्रुतोऽहमदृष्टोऽहमन्वेष्टव्योऽमरोऽस्म्यहम् || ८५ ||

adṛśyo'hamavarṇo'hamakhaṇḍo'smyahamadbhutaḥ |
aśruto'hamadṛṣṭo'hamanveṣṭavyo'maro'smyaham || 85 ||

अवायुरप्यनाकाशोऽतेजस्कोऽव्यभिचार्यहम् |
अमतोऽहमजातोऽहमतिसूक्ष्मोऽविकार्यहम् || ८६ ||

avāyurapyanākāśo'tejasko'vyabhicāryaham |
amato'hamajāto'hamatisūkṣmo'vikāryaham || 86 ||

अरजस्कोऽतमस्कोऽहमसत्त्वोऽस्म्यगुणोऽस्म्यहम् |
अमायोऽनुभवात्माहमनन्योऽविषयोऽस्म्यहम् || ८७ ||

arajasko'tamasko'hamasattvosmyaguṇo'smyaham |
amāyo'nubhavātmāhamananyo'viṣayo'smyaham || 87 ||

अद्वैतोऽहमपूर्णोऽहमबाह्योऽहमनन्तरः |
अश्रोतोऽहमदीर्घोऽहमव्यक्तोऽहमनामयः || ८८ ||

advaito'hamapūrṇo'hamabāhyo'hamanantaraḥ |
aśroto'hamadīrgho'hamavyakto'hamanāmayaḥ || 88||

अद्वयानन्दविज्ञानघनोऽस्म्यहमविक्रियः |
अनिच्छोऽहमलेपोऽहमकर्तास्म्यहमद्वयः || ८९||

advayānandavijñānaghano'smyahamavikriyaḥ |
aniccho'hamalepo'hamakartāsmyahamadvayaḥ || 89||

अविद्याकार्यहीनोऽहमवाग्रसनगोचरः |
अनल्पोऽहमशोकोऽहमविकल्पोऽस्म्यविज्वलन् || ९०||

avidyākāryahīno'hamavāgrasanagocaraḥ |
analpo'hamaśoko'hamavikalpo'smyavijvalan || 90||

आदिमध्यान्तहीनोऽहमाकाशसदृशोऽस्म्यहम् |
आत्मचैतन्यरूपोऽहमहमानन्दचिद्घनः || ९१||

ādimadhyāntahīno'hamākāśasadṛśo'smyaham |
ātmacaitanyarūpo'hamahamānandacidghanaḥ || 91||

आनन्दामृतरूपोऽहमात्मसंस्थोहमन्तरः |
आत्मकामोहमाकाशात्परमात्मेश्वरोऽस्म्यहम् || ९२||

ānandāmṛtarūpo'hamātmasaṃsthohamantaraḥ |
ātmakāmohamākāśātparamātmeśvarosmyaham || 92||

ईशानोऽस्म्यहमीड्योऽहमहमुत्तमपूरुषः |
उत्कृष्टोऽहमुपद्रष्टा अहमुत्तरतोऽस्म्यहम् || ९३||

īśānosmyahamīḍyo'hamahamuttamapūruṣaḥ |
utkṛṣṭo'hamupadraṣṭā ahamuttarato'smyaham || 93||

केवलोऽहं कविः कर्माध्यक्षोऽहं करणाधिपः ।
गुहाशयोऽहं गोप्ताहं चक्षुष्ष्चक्षुरस्म्यहम् ॥ ९४॥

kevalo'haṃ kaviḥ karmādhyakṣo'haṃ karaṇādhipaḥ |
guhāśayo'haṃ goptāhaṃ cakṣuṣaścakṣurasmyaham || 94||

चिदानन्दोऽस्म्यहं चेता चिद्घनश्चिन्मयोऽस्म्यहम् ।
ज्योतिर्मयोऽस्म्यहं ज्यायाञ्ज्योतिषां ज्योतिरस्म्यहम् ॥ ९५॥

cidānando'smyahaṃ cetā cidghanaścinmayo'smyaham |
jyotirmayo'smyahaṃ jyāyāñjyotiṣāṃ jyotirasmyaham || 95||

तमसः साक्ष्यहं तुर्यतुर्योऽहं तमसः परः ।
दिव्यो देवोऽस्मि दुर्दर्शो दृष्टाध्यायो ध्रुवोऽस्म्यहम् ॥ ९६॥

tamasaḥ sākṣyahaṃ turyaturyo'haṃ tamasaḥ paraḥ |
divyo devo'smi durdarśo dṛṣṭādhyāyo dhruvo'smyaham || 96||

नित्योऽहं निरवद्योऽहं निष्क्रियोऽस्मि निरञ्जनः ।
निर्मलो निर्विकल्पोऽहं निराख्यातोऽस्मि निश्चलः ॥ ९७॥

nityo'haṃ niravadyo'haṃ niṣkriyo'smi nirañjanaḥ |
nirmalo nirvikalpo'haṃ nirākhyāto'smi niścalaḥ || 97||

निर्विकारो नित्यपूतो निर्गुणो निःस्पृहोऽस्म्यहम् ।
निरिन्द्रियो नियन्ताहं निरपेक्षोऽस्मि निष्कलः ॥ ९८॥

nirvikāro nityapūto nirguṇo niḥspṛho'smyaham |
nirindriyo niyantāhaṃ nirapekṣo'smi niṣkalaḥ || 98||

पुरुषः परमात्माहं पुराणः परमोऽस्म्यहम् ।
परावरोऽस्म्यहं प्राज्ञः प्रपञ्चोपशमोऽस्म्यहम् ॥ ९९॥

puruṣaḥ paramātmāhaṃ purāṇaḥ paramo'smyaham |
parāvaro'smyahaṃ prājñaḥ prapañcopaśamo'smyaham || 99||

परामृतोऽस्म्यहं पूर्णः प्रभुरस्मि पुरातनः ।
पूर्णानन्दैकबोधोऽहं प्रत्यगेकरसोऽस्म्यहम् ॥ १००॥

parāmṛto'smyahaṃ pūrṇaḥ prabhurasmi purātanaḥ |
pūrṇānandaikabodho'haṃ pratyagekaraso'smyaham || 100||

प्रज्ञातोऽहं प्रशान्तोऽहं प्रकाशः परमेश्वरः ।
एकदा चिन्त्यमानोऽहं द्वैताद्वैतविलक्षणः ॥ १०१॥

prajñāto'haṃ praśānto'haṃ prakāśaḥ parameśvaraḥ |
ekadā cintyamāno'haṃ dvaitādvaitavilakṣaṇaḥ || 101||

बुद्धोऽहं भूतपालोऽहं भारूपो भगवानहम् ।
महाज्ञेयो महानस्मि महाज्ञेयो महेश्वरः ॥ १०२॥

buddho'haṃ bhūtapālo'haṃ bhārūpo bhagavānaham |
mahājñeyo mahānasmi mahājñeyo maheśvaraḥ || 102||

विमुक्तोऽहं विभुरहं वरेण्यो व्यापकोऽस्म्यहम् ।
वैश्वानरो वासुदेवो विश्वतश्चक्षुरस्म्यहम् ॥ १०३॥

vimukto'ham vibhuraham vareṇyo vyāpako'smyaham |
vaiśvānaro vāsudevo viśvataścakṣurasmyaham || 103 ||

विश्वाधिकोऽहं विशदो विष्णुर्विश्वकृदस्म्यहम् ।
शुद्धोऽस्मि शुक्रः शान्तोऽस्मि शाश्वतोऽस्मि शिवोऽस्म्यहम् ॥ १०४ ॥

viśvādhiko'ham viśado viṣṇurviśvakṛdasmyaham |
śuddho'smi śukraḥ śānto'smi śāśvato'smi śivo'smyaham || 104 ||

सर्वभूतान्तरात्महमहमस्मि सनातनः ।
अहं सकृद्विभातोऽस्मि स्वे महिम्नि सदा स्थितः ॥ १०५ ॥

sarvabhūtāntarātmahamahamasmi sanātanaḥ |
aham sakṛdvibhāto'smi sve mahimni sadā sthitaḥ || 105 ||

सर्वान्तरः स्वयंज्योतिः सर्वाधिपतिरस्म्यहम् ।
सर्वभूताधिवासोऽहं सर्वव्यापी स्वराडहम् ॥ १०६ ॥

sarvāntaraḥ svayamjyotiḥ sarvādhipatirasmyaham |
sarvabhūtādhivāso'ham sarvavyāpī svarāḍaham || 106 ||

समस्तसाक्षी सर्वात्मा सर्वभूतगुहाशयः ।
सर्वेन्द्रियगुणाभासः सर्वेन्द्रियविवर्जितः ॥ १०७ ॥

samastasākṣī sarvātmā sarvabhūtaguhāśayaḥ |
sarvendriyaguṇābhāsaḥ sarvendriyavivarjitaḥ || 107 ||

स्थानत्रयव्यतीतोऽहं सर्वानुग्राहकोऽस्म्यहम् ।
सच्चिदानन्द पूर्णात्मा सर्वप्रेमास्पदोऽस्म्यहम् ॥ १०८ ॥

sthānatrayavyatīto'ham sarvānugrāhako'smyaham |
saccidānanda pūrṇātmā sarvapremāspado'smyaham || 108 ||

सच्चिदानन्दमात्रोऽहं स्वप्रकाशोऽस्मि चिद्धनः ।
सत्त्वस्वरूपसन्मात्रसिद्धसर्वात्मकोऽस्म्यहम् ॥ १०९॥

saccidānandamātro'haṃ svaprakāśo'smi cidghanaḥ ।
sattvasvarūpasanmātrasiddhasarvātmako'smyaham ॥ 109॥

सर्वाधिष्ठानसन्मात्रः स्वात्मबन्धहरोऽस्म्यहम् ।
सर्वग्रासोऽस्म्यहं सर्वद्रष्टा सर्वानुभूरहम् ॥ ११०॥

sarvādhiṣṭhānasanmātraḥ svātmabandhaharo'smyaham ।
sarvagrāso'smyahaṃ sarvadraṣṭā sarvānubhūraham ॥ 110॥

---

*The real form of the atman to be contemplated upon by
the hamsa-yogin*

I am the manifestation of the senses and their Gunas, and devoid of all senses
I have my seat beyond the three states (waking, sleeping, and dreaming) I
bestow my favour on all. Then, it goes on to explain the eight Gunas of Atma
we saw in the conclusion, Apahatapapma ......

एवं यो वेद तत्त्वेन स वै पुरुष उच्यत इत्युपनिषत् ॥

evaṃ yo veda tattvena sa vai puruṣa ucyata ityupaniṣat ॥

ॐ सह नाववतु ॥ सह नौ भुनक्तु ॥ सह वीर्यं करवावहै ॥

oṃ saha nāvavatu ॥ saha nau bhunaktu ॥ saha vīryaṃ karavāvahai ॥

तेजस्विनावधीतमस्तु मा विद्विषावहै ॥

tejasvināvadhītamastu mā vidviṣāvahai ॥

ॐ शान्तिः शान्तिः शान्तिः ॥

14. Exhibit-2- Bramha-Vidya Panchakam

(Five verses on the Bramhan Lore) by Sree Narayana Guru

A series on Bramha vidya Panchakam of Sree Narayana Guru is shown below. In this series, he is sharing the five original Sanskrit verses of Bramha vidya Panchakam one by one with their English transliteration and at their translation and explanation in English.

Verse 1:

नित्यानित्यविवेकतो हि नितराम्
निर्वेदमापद्य सद्-
विद्वानत्र शमादिषड्कलसितः
स्यान्मुक्तिकामो भुवि;
पश्चाद् ब्रह्मविदुत्तमं प्रणतिसे-
वाद्यैः प्रसन्नं गुरुम्
पृच्छेत् कोऽहमिदं कुतो जगदिति
स्वामिन् वद त्वं प्रभो! ।।१।।

English Transliteration:
Nityānityavivekato hi nitarām
nirvedamāpadya sad-
vidvānatra Śamādishadkalasitaḥ
syānmuktikāmo bhuvi ;
paśchād Bramha viduttamam pranatise-
vadyaiḥ prasannam gurum
pṛcchet koŚhamidam kuto jagaditi
Swāmin vada tvam Prabho! – (1)

English Translation:
By discrimination between the eternal and the ephemeral, attaining to high dispassion, the well-versed one, Shining with the six-fold qualifications of shama, etc.,
Becomes desirous of liberation here in this world. He, then, approaching a

great Knower of the Absolute – Guru, and pleasing him with prostrations, services, etc., Should ask thus, "'Who am I?', 'Wherefrom came the world?' O Master! O Lord! Do Thou convey." – (1)

Verse 2:

त्वं हि ब्रह्म न चेन्द्रियाणि न मनो
बुद्धिर्न चित्तं वपुः
प्राणाहङ्कृतयोऽन्यदप्यसदवि-
द्या कल्पितं स्वात्मनि
सर्वं दृश्यतया जडं जगदिदं
त्वत्तः परं नान्यतो
जातं न स्वत एव भाति मृगतृ-
ष्णाभं दरीदृश्यताम् ॥२॥

English Transliteration:
Tvam hi Bramhana cendriyāni na mano
Budhirna cittam vapuḥ
PrānahaṅkṛtayoSnyadapyasadavi-
dyā kalpitam svātmani
Sarvam dṛśyatayā jaḍam jagadidam
Tvattaḥ param nānyato
Jātam na svata eva bhāti mṛgatṛ-
ṣnābham daridṛśyatām. – **(2)**

English Translation:
Thou verily art Bramha n, and not the senses,
Neither the mind nor the intellect,
Neither the chitta nor the body,
Others such as the prana, I-sense, etc. too
Are unreal and super-imposed by avidya on the Self.
Being drishya (seen), inert is this whole world,
Neither born of anything apart from you,
Nor manifesting by itself,
Apparent like the mirage,
May this be well-discerned! – (2)

Verse 3:
व्याप्तं येन चराचरं घटशरा-
वादीव मृत्सत्तया

यस्यान्तःस्फुरितमं यदात्मकमिदं
जातं यतो वर्तते;
यस्मिन् यत् प्रलये पि सद्घनमजं
सर्वं यदन्वेति तत्
सत्यं विद्ध्यमृताय निर्मलधियो
यस्मै नमस्कुर्वते ।।३।।

English Transliteration:
Vyāptaṁ yena carācaraṁ ghataśarā-
vādiva mṛtsattayā
yasyāntaḥsphuritaṁ yadātmakamidaṁ
jātam yato vartate
yasmiṅ yat pralayeɔpi sadghanamajaṁ
sarvaṁ yadanveti tat
satyam viddhyamṛtāya nirmaladhiyo
yasmai namaskurvate – (3)

English Translation:
That, by which the living and the non-living are pervaded
Like the pot, jug, etc. by clay substance,
That, within which this (world) shines,
That, which this in essence is,
That, from which this was born,
That, in which this exists,
That, which continues as Pure Being Unborn even during dissolution,
That, which follows everything (Omnipresent),
Know That to be the Reality, the Eternal,
To which the pure in mind pay their obeisance. – (3)

Verse 4:
सृष्ट्वेदं प्रकृतेरनुप्रविशती
येयं यया धार्यते।
प्राणीति प्रविविक्तभुग्बहिरहं
प्राज्ञस्सुषुप्तौ यतः
यस्यामात्मकला स्फुरत्यहमिति
प्रत्यन्तरङ्गं जनैः
यस्यै स्वस्ति समर्थ्यते प्रतिपदा
पूर्णा शृणु त्वं हि सा।।४।।

72

English Transliteration:
Sṛṣṭvedam prakṛteranupraviśati-
yeyaṁ yaya dhāryate
prāṇiti praviviktabhugbahirahaṁ
prājnassusuptau yataḥ
yasyamātmakala sphuratyahamiti
pratyantarangam janaiḥ
yasyai svasti samarthyate pratipada
pūrna shṛnu tvam hi sa. – (4)

English Translation:
She, who after having created this (world) from her own nature,
Entered into it Herself,
She, by whom this is held,
She, by whom the living being acts externally as 'I',
As the experiencer in the dream-state,

And as 'Prājna' (प्रज्ञ) in deep sleep,

She, whose self-fragment pulsates as 'I' in each heart,
She, to whom glory is declared by the people,
She, who is complete in each stride,
Listen! Thou indeed art She! – (4)

Verse 5:
प्रज्ञानं त्वहमस्मि तत्त्वमसि तद्
ब्रह्मायमात्मेति सं-
गायन् विप्रचरप्रशान्तमनसा
त्वं ब्रह्मबोधोदयात्।
प्रारब्धं क्व नु सञ्चितं तव किमा-
गामि क्व कर्माप्यसत्
त्वय्यध्यस्तमतोऽखिलं त्वमसि स-
च्चिन्मात्रमेकं विभुः ॥५॥

English Transliteration:
Prajnānaṁ tvahamasmi tattvamasi tad
brahmāyamātmeti saṁ-
gāyan vipracara praśāntamanasa
tvam Bramha bodhodayāt
prārabdhaṁ kvanu sanchitaṁ tava kimā
gāmi kva karmāpyasat

tvayyadhyastamato'khilam tvamasi sa-
ccinmatramekam vibhuḥ – (5)

English Translation:
'Consciousness indeed am I, 'That thou art,
'That Bramha n is this Self' – thus singing ever,
Do thou roam around blissfully with a peaceful mind
Resulting from the dawn of knowledge of the Bramha n,
Where then is Prarabdha for thou?
What Sanchita and where is Agami for thou?
Karma itself is non-existent,
On thou, superimposed are all these,
Thou therefore art Being-Consciousness Non-dual Omnipresence alone. – (5)

15. Exhibit-3- ब्रह्म सूक्तं

(From TAITREEYA BRAMHA NA(TB) 2.8.8.10, 2.8.8.11)

This is a set of mantras in the Taittiriya Bramha na Yajurveda, which are dedicated to praising the Supreme Being, Bramhan. The mantras are mentioned, in TB 2.8.8.10 and TB 2.8.8.11, The mantra is also known as the Bramha Suktam. It is a hymn in praise of Bramhan, the ultimate reality in Sanatana DharmA

Here are the mantras along with their meanings:

ब्रह्म जज्ञानं प्रथमं पुरस्तात्| वि सीमत स्सुरुचो वेन आवः|| स बुद्धि्नया उपमा अस्य विष्ठाः | सतश्च योनि मसतश्च विवः|| पिता विराजामृषभो रयीणां | अन्तरिक्षं विश्वरूप आविवेश || तमर्कैरभ्यर्च्चन्ति वत्सं| ब्रह्मसन्तं ब्रह्मणा वर्द्धयन्तः|| ब्रह्म देवा नजनयत् | ब्रह्म विश्वमिदं जगत् || ब्रह्मणः क्षत्रं निर्मितं | ब्रह्म ब्रह्मण आत्मना || अन्तरस्मिन्निमे लोकाः | अन्तर्विश्वमिदं जगत् | ब्रह्मैव भूतानां ज्येष्ठं| तेन कोऽर्हति स्पर्द्धितुं || ब्रह्मं देवास्त्रयस्त्रिशत् | ब्रह्मन्निन्द्र प्रजापती | ब्रह्मन् ह विश्वा भूतानि | नावीवान्त स्समाहिता || चतस आशाः प्रचरन्त्वग्नय : | इमन्नो यज्ञन्नयतु प्रजानन् | घृतं पिन्वन्नजर सुवीरं| ब्रह्म समिद् भवत्याहुतीनाम् ||

Here is the meaning:

ब्रह्म जज्ञानं प्रथमं पुरस्तात् | Bramhan (the Ultimate Reality) is the first and foremost knowledge.

वि सीमत स्सुरुचो वेन आवः || His form is limitless, and He pervades everything.

स बुद्धि्नया उपमा अस्य विष्ठाः | He is indescribable and His greatness cannot be compared.

सतश्च योनि मसतश्च विवः || He exists both as the cause and effect of all that is.

पिता विराजामृषभो रयीणां | He is the father of all beings and the most radiant one.

अन्तरिक्षं विश्वरूप आविवेश || He pervades the entire universe and its vast expanse.

तमर्कैरभ्यर्च्चन्ति वत्सं | Even the gods worship Him with great reverence.

ब्रह्मसन्तं ब्रह्मणा वर्द्धयन्तः || The sages and seers extol Him and worship Him.

ब्रह्म देवा नजनयत् | All the gods were born from Him.

ब्रह्म विश्वमिदं जगत् || He is the creator of the entire universe.

ब्रह्मणः क्षत्रं निर्मितं | He created the Kshatriya (warrior) caste.

ब्रह्म ब्रह्मण आत्मना || He created Brahmins (priests) and Himself became the Self of all beings.

अन्तरस्मिन्निमे लोकाः | All the worlds exist within Him.

अन्तर्विश्वमिदं जगत् | He is the inner controller of the universe.

ब्रह्मैव भूतानां ज्येष्ठं| Bramha n is the greatest among all beings.

तेन कोऽर्हति स्पर्द्धितुं || Who can compete with Him?

ब्रह्मं देवास्त्रयस्त्रिशत् | The gods worship Him with thirty-three hymns.

ब्रह्मन्निन्द्र प्रजापती | Indra and Prajapati (the creator) are aspects of Bramha n.

16. Conclusion

PratyagAtma and ParamAtmA-

The secret of Bramha vidyā is to reveal the real nature of the Ātmā, that is all-pervading, that is like ghee in the milk, that is the source of <u>Atmavidyā</u> and <u>Tapas</u> and to show that everything is in essence one. This is the English translation of the Bramha Upanishad (belonging to the Krishna-Yajurveda). (From Sri. Narayanaswamy's transliteration of Bramha Vidya from the book "Thirty Minor Upanishads" published in the Year 1914.

According to Vishishtadvaita philosophy Surrender (NyAsA) as stated is the best option for JivA for Liberation.

I will narrate here another Important AcharyA **Sri.Alawandar's** (Sri RAmAnUjA's Guru) Storaratna and what he says about NyAsA.

Sri NaTamuni and Sri Yamuna occupy a central position (*Natha-Yamuna madhyamam*) among the illustrious Acharyas, who reformed and revitalized the ancient system of thought and faith – *Vishitadvaita Siddantha*

Sri Ramanuja inherited that rich heritage; and enhanced it further. It was on the basis of the works of his Grand Acharya (*PrAchAryA**) *i. e.*, Sri Yamunacharya, that Sri Ramanuja, later, established, fortified and perfected the *Vishistadvaita Siddantha.* [*Sri Yamunacharya was said to be the preceptor of Mahāpūrṇa who initiated Sri RaamAnujA.]

17. Stotra-Ratnam

(Entire 65 slokAs and Meanings are annexed in exhibit-4 of this book for Reader's delight)

Stotra-Ratna and Chatus-sloki are hymns singing the glory and splendour of Lord Vishnu and Devi Lakshmi. They are the fervent outpouring of Sri Yamuna's intense devotion towards Vishnu and Lakshmi; and, his deep-rooted longing for communion with his favourite deity

The Stotra-Ratna is a garland of sixty-five -verse hymns submitted to the lotus feet of Lord Vishnu in the spirit of **Sharanagati or complete surrender seeking Moksha.** These hymns, in delightfully lucid verses, present the central philosophical theme and outlook of VishishtAdvaita doctrine, elucidating its essential principles of Tattva (the intricate relation between God, nature and human); Hita (the excellent path that leads to ones' emancipation); and, PurushArthA (the attainment of the supreme goal).

It is said; Sri Vedanta Desika was deeply moved and highly inspired by the <u>28th Sloka of the Stotra- Ratna</u>, which extols the virtues of submitting to the Lord, in intense devotion, enormous reverence and deep humility, with folded hands (anjali mudra).

Anjali mudra in front of Bramha n the supreme god

(Whosoever, in whatever manner, at whatever time, supplicates to You with palms joined even once, that act dispels at once all his miseries and contributes to his well-being. An act of supplication to You is never in vain-SlokA 22 of Storaratna-Exhibit-2). The Observance of Prapatthi (NyAsA) (slOkam 22), Swami Desikan's analysis of the architectonics of this Stotram-Exhibit-2

न धर्मनिष्ठोऽस्मि न चात्मवेदि
न भक्तिमान् त्वच्चरणारविन्दे।
अकिञ्चनोऽनन्यगतिः शरण्य!

तवत्पादमूलं शरणं प्रपद्ये ।।२२।।

Oh, Supreme Being! Even if You drive me away, I cannot relinquish Your Lotus-feet; a suckling does not at all desire to leave its mother's feet at any time, even if it has been set aside by her in anger. SlokA26

nirāsakasyāpi na tāvadutsahē
mahēśa hātuṁ tava pādapaṅkajam.
ruSā nirastō'pi śiśuḥ stanandhavō
na jātu mātuścaraṇau jihāsati ।।26।।

त्व दङ्घ्रिमुद्दिश्य कदापि केनचिध्यथा
तथावाऽपि सक्त्कृतोऽञ्चलिः |
तदैवमुष्णात्य शुभान्यशेषत -
शुभानि पुष्णाति न जातु हीयते

tva daṅghrimuddiśya kadāpi kēnacidhyathā
tathāvā'pi saktkṛtō'ñcaliḥ |
tadaivamuṣṇātya śubhānyaśēṣata -
subhaani puhNaati na jaatu hiiyate।।28।।

Meaning of Sloka 28:

Oh Lord! When one submits to your sacred feet, with devotion and humility, as Upayam (means) and Phalam (fruit, result) with folded hands (anjali mudra), even once, his past ill-fated Karmas would soon be destroyed; it would secure freedom from every sort of fear; and, he would enjoy the blessed joy of residing in your supreme abode of Sri Vaikunta. Such submissions to you with folded hands will surely bring all auspiciousness into one's life.

It is said; when Sri Desika pondered over the essence of this (28th) verse of the Stotra-Ratna, he was struck by the awe-inspiring significance and the immense auspiciousness of this simple gesture of submitting to the Lord with folded hands (*Anjali*) in a spirit of absolute surrender (**Sharanagati, Prapatti**). And, that inspired him to annotate its verse 28 ; to give a detailed exposition of its essence; and, to compose his, now famous, garland of verses under the title *Anjali-Vibhavam* (the glory and splendour of *Anjali*).

Further, it is also said; that Sri Ramanuja was much moved by recitation of the *Stotra-Ratna*; and, that inspired him to compose the *Vaikunta-Gatyam*, a pure expression of Bhakti immersed in the spirit of *Atma-Nivarana*. –

(From -https://sreenivasaraos.com/tag/siddhi-traya/)

PrajApati and eight Qualities of Atma (Refer Ch 5, 6 RamAnujA's Explanation of PrajApati VAkyam)

Again and again the <u>Upaniṣads</u> glorify Self-knowledge, but what is the nature of the Self, and how do we attain that knowledge? Here the <u>Upaniṣad</u> begins a story to answer this. Once Prajāpati, the creator, decided to teach people about the Self. He described the Self as *apahata-pāpmā*, free from sins, or blemishes (*pāpa*)—that is to say, it is pure. *Vijara*—it never ages, or decays. *Vimṛtyu*—it is free from death.

य आत्मापहतपाप्मा विजरो विमृत्युर्विशोको विजिघत्सोऽपिपासः सत्यकामः सत्यसंकल्पः सोऽन्वेष्टव्यः स विजिज्ञासितव्यः स सर्वांश्च लोकानाप्नोति सर्वांश्च कामान्यस्तमात्मनमनुविद्य विजानातीति ह प्रजापतिरुवाच||

(छा. उप. ८.७.१) (This is explained under PrajApati Vakyam Page 10,11 title No-5,6)

ya ātmāpahatapāpmā vijarō vimṛtyurviśōkō vijighatsō'pipāsaḥ satyakāmaḥ satyasaṃkalpaḥ sō'nveṣṭavyaḥ sa vijijñāsitavyaḥ sa sarvāṃśca lōkānāpnōti sarvāṃśca kāmānyastamātmanamanuvidya vijānātīti ha prajāpatiruvāca|| (chā. upa. 8.7.1)

Word by word meaning

1.Yaḥ <u>ātmā</u> apahatapāpmā- the Self is free from sin;

2.vijaraḥ-free from the effects of age;

3.vimṛtyuḥ-free from death;

4.<u>viśokaḥ</u>- free from sorrow;

5.vijighatsaḥ- free from hunger;

6.apipāsaḥ- free from thirst;

7.<u>satyakāmaḥ</u>- is the cause of desire for Truth;

8.satyasaṅkalpaḥ- is the cause of commitment to Truth;

saḥ, that;

anveṣṭavyaḥ- has to be sought;

saḥ vijijñāsitavyaḥ- that has to be thoroughly investigated;

saḥ- a person;

sarvān ca lokān āpnoti- attains all worlds;

sarvān ca kāmān- and all desires;

yaḥ- who;

tam ātmānam, that Self;

anuvidya-having learned;

 vijānāti- [and] knows it;

prajāpatiḥ iti ha uvāca- Prajāpati said so.

The body, of course, is subject to decay and it perishes. When you look at an old person you can tell at once that the body has decayed. It has become weak, and there are wrinkles and grey hair, and so on. Then gradually it must perish. That which has birth also has death. No matter when the body was born, it will eventually begin to fall apart and die. But the Self will never die. Then Prajāpati says, the Self is *viśoka*, without sorrow, *vijighatsa*, not subject to hunger, and *apipāsa*, not subject to thirst. Besides this, the Self is *satyakāma* and *satyasaṅkalpa*—seeking the Truth and always rooted in Truth. That is to say, it is Truth- (ज्ञानम्) itself. It is always one with Truth, so it can never deviate from Truth.

"Saḥ anveṣṭavyaḥ"—that has to be known. **This is the purpose of life**. Sri Ramakrishna used to say, **'To realize God is the goal of life.'** The goal is not money, not power, not scholarship. It is nothing but God. *Saḥ vijijñāsitavyaḥ*—**it has to be enquired about**. You cannot sit back and wait for it to reveal itself to you. You must go and find someone to teach you about it. And when you have found a capable teacher, you must fall at his feet and beg him to teach you. Then you must ask again and again until your doubts are removed: 'Is it like this? Is it like that?' But you must go to someone who knows the Self. Can a blind man lead another blind man? If the teacher does not know the Self, how will you learn?

When you fulfil these conditions, what happens? You get everything you want. You become supreme. The **Upaniṣad says, you conquer the whole universe. How? In this way too, all your desires are fulfilled**. Self-knowledge gives you the step to realize the highest, supreme God, the Bramha m. You may have everything else—friends, relatives, great political power, money, scholarship, a high social standing—but if you do not have Self-knowledge, Bramha m's knowledge and the relation between these two, everything is useless. Prajāpati has declared: ' 'Come and learn from me.' Here, in order to

teach the nature of the Self, and Bramha n, and also to emphasize the need for self-discipline to attain Self-knowledge one must find a Guru and take Upadesam from him.

NyAsa VidyA

Bramha SutrA 3.3.56 and 3.3.57 speaks up the following:

Despite different means of UpAsanA in the thirty-two VidyAs, there is a freedom of choice in regard to DhyAnA. The outcome of results would be same and there is no difference in the same. In order to reach Bramha n after realsing the self there are two routes:

1.Bakthi, 2. Prapatti. Both are independent routes to attaining liberation (MokshA-realisation of Bramha m). However, NyAsa is excellent and preferred route. AtmA already has the above eight qualities as potential, and are manifested when this Liberation(MokshA) happens. Bakthi YogA is a steep and difficult path since it cannot be practised easily by everyone. Sri. Bagavat RamAnujA in his Gita Bhashyam while expresses the meaning of :

सर्वधर्मान्परित्यज्य मामेकं शरणं व्रज |

अहं त्वां सर्वपापेभ्यो मोक्षयिष्यामि मा शुच: || BG. 18.66||

sarva-dharmān parityajya mām ekaṁ śharaṇaṁ vraja   /

ahaṁ tvāṁ sarva-pāpebhyo mokṣhayiṣhyāmi mā śhuchaḥ //

says,

Since Bagavat Gita is a Bakthi Yoga grantha, this sloka is only to surrender to God and seek, Bakthi YogA ends without any hinderance. However, in His SaraNAgati Gatyam He surrenders to Lord RanganathA and ThAyAr, and shows us the path to MokshA is simple, by Prapatti only. Swami Desikan also expresses this is "the Tiruvullam (This Prapatti is in His mind) of Sri. Bagavat RamAnujA, and advocates Prapatti is preferred to Bakthi. (Kalakshepam of Ahobila Mutt AstAna Vidwan Vaikunta Vasi Sri. Mannarkudi RajagopalAchAriAr) Prapatti is said as "NyAsa VidyA in Bramha UpAsanam.

NyAsa-VidyA requies a deep desire to attain Lord's feet (MokshA) and the firm faith and belief in His protective ability(रक्षगत्वम्) by a JivA. Also, other requirements are, to express his utter helplessness to follow any other form of YogA to attain self- realisation followed by realisation of Bramha m. There are five AngAs along with one Angi- Surrender (the Sixth) and Swami Desikan in His Rahasya Traya Saram, Chapter -4, Artha PancakA-advocates, that Artha Pancakam or ShadArtham are not different. The Artha PancakAs are five elements a JivA should know by Bramha VidyA through a Guru (AchAryA) and they are:

1. To know about Bramha Swaroopam,
2. To know about Jiva Swaroopm
3. What is UpAyam for Moksha (both UpAyam and UpEyam are Sriman NarAyaNA)
4. Result of this DhyAnam-i.e., Moksham (Realisation of Bramha m)
5. Enemy for MokshA PrApti and Remedy for the same.
6. The sixth one is total Surrender of AtmA itself to Bramha m.

After understanding the Five AngAs actual surrender to Bramha m with the help of a Guru is the Angi.

82

How NyAsa VidyA is performed:

Essence of NyAsa VidyA is to surrender completely to Bramha m with the help of a Guru, and enter-into His Kainkaryam (SevA- serve Him in all possible ways). NyAsa vidyA says: NyAsa, the surrender to Bramha m is the highest form of everything one could do. To leave SamsArA, surrender, and submit to Him all our responsibilities and burden (भार) is NyAsa. NyAsa, the surrender to Bramha m is the highest form of everything says this VidyA:

न्यास इत्याहुः मनीषिणो ब्रह्माणं ब्रह्मा विश्वः कतमः स्वयम्भुः प्रजापतिः संवतथ्सर इति॥

nyāsa ityāhuḥ manīṣiṇō brahmānaṁ brahmā viśvaḥ katamaḥ svayambhuḥ prajāpatiḥ saṁvatsara iti. | |

ब्रह्मणे त्वा महस ओमित्यात्मानं युञ्जीतैतद्वै महोपनिषदम्|

Bramha ṇē tvā mahasa āōmityātmānaṁ yuñjītaitadvai mahōpaniṣadam |

nyAsa VidyA recommends, that in order to liberate and attain MokshA, a jiVa must understsnd that Bramha m is the means and Bramha m is the Goal also. Then like PraNavA mantrA is used in yAgA for committed devotion of putting DravyA in YagA, one has to give away his own Atma (Prtyag-AtmA) to Him.

Post Prapatti- (NyAsA) how one should conduct is spelt out in detail by Swami Desikan in His, Rahasya traya sAram. One has to consider the entire Life and follow the same as a YogA, and await the day when he will leave SamsArA and this world to travel to the location where Bramha m is situated. (Vaikuntam) through ArchirAdhi Marga (Path). **From this we know that NyAsa VidyA is an easier alternative to Bakthi YogA.**

18. Exhibit-4 -Stotra Ratnam

Introduction:

YAAMUNA'S STHOTHRA RATNAM:

After completing the Chathussloki on the MahAthmyam of Sri Devi, AaLavandhAr proceeded to compose his tribute to Sriman NarayaNa. There are 65 slOkAs in this sthothram. The number 65 is the sum of the letters contained in the three Rahasyams (Rahasya Traya Saram)

Therefore, Stotra Ratnam is considered the essence of Rahasya Trayam or it is the Rahasya traya SAram.

It has been said that there is no KavyA that moves one's heart as Srimath RaamayaNam; similarly, Stotra-Ratnam has been considered by PurvAchAryAs as the sthothram that is matchless in moving one's heart. It has profound philosophical principles and yet it is a moving appeal to the Lord and cries out for His grace. This Stotram is a great lesson in the stages that one must go through to perform SaraNAgathi and to become free of fear about SamsAra.

The sthothram starts and ends in the traditional way of salutations to one's AchArya. Swami Desikan states that this gem of a stotram is placed in the beautiful box of Acharya sthuthi. YaamunA starts with the salutation to his Acharya and then moves on to praise BhagavAn. He becomes diffident about his qualifications for the task and yet wants to eulogize Him in the manner of

VedAs and Upanishads. His resolution gets diluted and he laments over his lack of qualifications and inadequacies and performs akinchana SaraNAgathi at the lotus feet of the Lord. He then comforts himself by reflecting that even a small upAyam such as SaraNAgathi can yield major auspicious results and that his goal in performing SaraNAgathi is to do Nithya Kaimkaryam in Sri Vaikuntam. He recognizes that the great sins that he has accumulated obstruct progress in the attainment of his desired goal. He states that he is however not discouraged as a result of his awareness of the Lord's DayA. He appeals movingly to the Lord to strengthen his SaraNAgathi efforts and to protect him from the obstacles that stand in his way towards the realization of his goal. He goes on to the next step of prayer, where he begs the Lord to grow his Bhakthi towards Him and to bless him to live with BhagavathAs and to live in a state of KArpaNyam devoid of egotistic thoughts. He pleads with the Lord for Acharya Sambhandham to realize the fruits of the glorious Prapatthi and declares his MahA ViswAsam in the Lord's KshamA and AnukampA-Compassion -Sympathy (to bless him with the fruits of Prapatthi.)

The meaning of Dhvayam is deftly interlaced in the body of this gem among Stotrams composed by AaLavandhAr. In the previous work, Chathussloki, our Acharya made Purushakaara Prapatthi (Requesting recommendation to God) to Sri Devi. Thereafter, as he starts to perform BharanyAsam at the holy feet of the Lord, he completes guru paramparAnusanthAnam as the first step as a prerequisite.

He elaborates next on the meaning of NaarAyaNa sabdham and follows the arc of Dhvayam and completes the SaraNAgathi at the sacred feet of Sriman NaarAyaNA. The second paadham of Dhvaya manthram comes into focus now. Our Acharya now explains the meaning of "SrimathE nArAyaNAya" section by stating that this portion stands for the obtainment of the fruit of nitya Kaimkaryam to Sri VaikunTa Nathan in Parama Padham. He adds next the slOkams that cover the "Nama:" section--the concluding word of Dhvayam - for seeking the Lord's anugraham to eliminate any leftover obstacles in his efforts to get the full benefits of SaraNAgathi (i.e.) Nitya Kaimkarya PurNAnubhavam. **Thus, the slOkams of Stotra Ratnam can be considered to cover the full meaning of the sacred Dhvaya Manthram**

THE GREATNESS OF ALAVANDHAR AND HIS WORKS

ALavandhAr (916-1041 A.D) was the grandson of NaTamuni (C 824-924 A.D), who recovered for posterity the Naalaaiyra Dhivya Prabhandham as a result of NammaazhwArs anugraham. ALavandhAr is also known as YaamunA Muni or YaamunAccharya. YAmunA is the grand-preceptor (PrAchAryA) of RaamAnujA. YAmunA established the principles of VishishtAdvaitam as an expansion of the doctrines housed in his grandfather's treatises: NyAya TattvA and Yoga RahasyA. He elaborated on those doctrines with authoritative scriptures such as Sruthis, Bhagavad Gita, AzhwAr's PAsurams and selected SAtvika PurAnAs. AaLavandhAr in the first verse of Chatussloki establishes the equal status of Sri Devi with Her consort. As Isvari of Sarva BhutAs, she enjoys an equal status and rules the physical and the transcendental universe. She possesses like Her Lord, Svarupam, Rupam, GuNam and Vibhavam. She shares in equal measure the six auspicious GuNAs of Her consort (BhagavAn): JnAnam, Bhalam, Sakthi, Iswaryam, Veeryam and Tejas. That is why she is known as Bhagavathi or ShAtgunya SampoorNai. She is always inseparable from her Lord and is stated as AnapAyini.

In the majestic fourth slOkam starting with the grand assembly of well-chosen words ripe with profound meanings -Saanthaananda Mahaa Vibhuthi Paramam Yadh Bramha Roopam Hare: …" and ends dramatically with the words "Aahu: svairanuroopa roopa vibhavai: GaaDopa gudaanitE". YaamunA asserts here that Sri Devis Roopams and GuNAs are tightly bonded together with that of Her Lord in an inseparable manner. Whenever He assumes Vyuha –Vibhava-HArtha-ArchA RoopAs. She takes the appropriate RupA and is tightly united with Him as AnapAyini. Thus, they demonstrate Eka Seshitvam and become UpAyam and Upeyam to us all.

Every slOkam of this StOtram houses the deep meanings of VedAntham (Upanishads). It is very difficult to understand the meanings of Upanishads thru the Upanishad texts alone. This problem is overcome however by studying the SthOthra Rathnam slOkams and understanding their meanings Swamy ALavandhAr's approach is to delight the minds of PaNDithaas and PaamarAs (common folks).

स्वादयन्निह सर्वेषां त्रय्यन्तार्थं सुदुर्ग्रहम् ।

स्तोत्रयामास योगीन्द्रः तं वन्दे यामुनाह्वयम्॥

svādayanniha sarvēṣām trayyantārtham sudurgrahama |

stōtrayāmāsa yōgīndramh tam vandē yāmunāhvayam | |

The composer of this Taniyan says: "adiyEn offers my salutations to Swamy ALavandhAr, who rendered such a great assistance (MahOpakAram). The key passages in this Taniyan are: "trayyanthArTam – sudurgraham" and "iha sarvEshAm svAdhayan strhOthrayAmAsa"

namō namō yāmunāya yāmunāya namaḥ   /

namō namō yāmunāya yāmunāya namō namaḥ   //

There are many **nama:** sabdhaas in this Taniyan. Each of the nama: sabdhAs have their own meanings. I salute Yaamuna Muni in Parama Padham for making it possible to reap the benefits of my **Prapatthi. (NyAsA- we speak in this Bramhavidya)** May the fruits of these namaskArams not belong to me, but only to **Him (The Bramham)** as the Seshi.

AaLavandhAr is also the author of two lyrical master pieces (stotra GranthAs) revered as Chathussloki and Stotra Ratnam. Latter is the forerunner of almost every Stotram composed by Acharyas such as of RAmAnujA, Kuresa, Parasara Bhattar, Swamy Desikan, MaNavALa Maamuni and others. Swami Desikan has written commentaries for both Chathussloki and Stotra Ratnam because of their importance to Sri VaishNava SiddAntham.

Swami Desikan's analysis of the architectonics of this Sthothram

Before focusing on the individual slOkaas of this magnificent and pioneering sthothram by AaLavandhAr, it may be interesting to study Swami Desikan's analysis of the architectonics of this sthothram. Swami starts off by stating that **YaamunA Muni composed Stotra Ratnam to house the rich meanings of Dhvaya manthram.** His analysis of the different sections that forms natural grouping of thoughts is as follows:

1. YaamunA salutes the Acharyas, who opened his spiritual eye (slOkams 1-5) and particularly his grandfather, RanganaTha Muni.

2. The sthothram proper begins in slOkam 6.

87

3. The awesome Parathvam of the Lord is hinted and the insufficiency and diffidence of the poet to tackle that profound subject of the Parathvam is indicated (slOkam 7).

4. The sowlabhyam of the Lord is invoked to overcome the fear of tackling such a profound task (SlOkams 8-9).

5. Elaboration of the **NaarAyana Sabdhaartham (SlOkams 10-21).**

6. **The Observance of Prapatthi (NyAsA) (slOkam 22).**

7. Declaration of his appropriateness (Svayogyaa Kathanam /adhikaaram) by YaamunA for the performance of his Prapatthi (slOkams 23-27).

8. **Statement of the fact that the simple-to-perform Prapatthi has disproportionately large dividends (slOkams 28-29).**

9. Revelation of the meaning of the uttara KanTam of Dhvayam as that which deals with the fruit of the Prapatthi (slOkams 30-46).

10. Expression of his regret over hitherto wasted days due to his lack of intensity to pursue the fruits of Prapatthi thru the observance of the appropriate Upaayam (slOkam 47). Nirvedam over his missed opportunities.

11. The importance of Mahaa Viswasam on the fruits to be gained by Prapatthi (slOkams 48- 51).

12. **Examination of the principles of Bara SamarpaNam (NyAsA) (slOkams 52-53).**

13. Prayer to give strength to observe strictly the conduct of post-prapanna life and sathsangam, while being on this earth (slOkams 54-57).

14. Statement on the Lord's kAruNyam, sambhandham (Bhandhutvam) as the hope for in the context of his Prapatthi (slOkam 58-63).

15. **Reminding the Lord of his saraNAgatha RakshaNa vratham of the Lord and prayer to include him in that vratham (slOkam 64).**

16. **Statement on the glories of the anugraham and sambhandham of the Acharya for successful Prapatthi and inclusion of his fearlessness (Nirbhayam) as a result of performing Prapatthi, even if he does not have the qualifications of his own (naicchiyAnusandhAnam)--slOkam 65 (final slokam).**

SlOkams and Commentaries:

SWAMY ALAVANDHAR'S STHOTHRA RATHNAM

(THE GEM OF HYMNS) ANNOTATED COMMENTARY IN ENGLISH BY:

OPPILIAPPAN KOIL SRI VARADACHARI SATHAKOPAN & MANNARGUDI SRI SRINIVASAN NARAYANAN

SlOkam 1

नमोऽचिन्त्याद्भुताक्लिष्ट ज्ञानवैराग्य राशये|
नाथाय मुनयेऽगाधभगवद् भक्तिसिन्दवे |१|

namō'cintyādbhutākliṣṭa jñānavairāgya rāśayē|
nāthāya munayē'gādhabhagavad bhaktisindavē |1|

Swamy Adidevananda's translation:

Obeisance to the contemplative saint NaTamuni, who is an unfathomable ocean of divine love and the embodiment of knowledge and renunciation – unthinkable, marvelous, and spontaneous.

Commentary:

Swamy NaaTa Muni is being saluted here by the poet-composer, ALavandhAr. NaaTa Muni's auspicious attributes are being explained: He is the embodiment of Jn~Anam and dispassion (VairAgyam). He is the abode of deep bhakthi for Sriman NaarAyaNA. His Jn~Anam and (VairAgyam)Virakthi are of the Caliber of "achinthyam, adhbutham and aklishtam". "Achinthyam" refers to the inability to describe in words or contemplate by the mind. It is not comparable to other saadhakaas' Jn~Anam or vairAgyam. It is beyond comprehension by our limited intellect and hence it is "adhbhutham". Swamy NaaTa Muni's Jn~Ana VairAgyam and Bhakthi was obtained by him effortlessly (without strain) because of the Lord's nirhEthuka krupA. All these qualities of Jn~Anam and VairAgyam are assembled together (Jn~Ana VairAgya Raasi) in NaaTa Muni. How is it so? Jn~Anam is constituted by many vishayams like the Lord's Roopam, Svaroopam, limitless guNams and VibhUthi (Iswaryam). The factors (vishayam) pertinent to Vairagyam again are a huge assembly such as Mother, Father, Children, land and innumerable earthly bhOgams. Therefore, it is appropriate to list these vishayams of Jn~Anam and VairAgyam as a RAsi or a huge pile or samooham.

Regarding Bhakthi Rasam, NaTa Muni is like a deep ocean, which has the quality of depth that makes it difficult to reach the floor. The deep ocean is also not perturbable and one cannot shake it through agitation (kadal kalakka mudiyAthathu). Swamy NaTa Muni had inside him the deep Bhagavath Bhakthi sAgaram. His name of NaaTa Muni suggests that he was a srEshta Muni (one who engages in unceasing meditation of the Lord). Swamy NaaTa Muni's Jn~Anam (ज्ञानम्) was Bhagavath prasAdha labdham (attained directly from BhagavAn:

This vilakshaNa Jn~Anam (ज्ञानम्) yielded dispassion (VairAgyam) to distaste for material things and samsAric relationships. Bhakthi has been defined as "snEha-poorva-anudhyAnam" and "SwAmini dhAsasya snEhamayee sTithi:" It is a state of unalloyed love for the Lord as His bonded servant. That is deep (aghAtha Bhagavath bhakthi). It also arises from Jn~Ana visEsham. Swamy NaaTa Muni was one of the rare "Bhagavath ParathvAnubhava janitha bhakthi paripoorNar" according to Swamy Desikan.

SlOkam 2

In this slOkam, ALavandhAr salutes many times his AchAryan's Acharyan (NaaTa Muni) in the manner referred to in VishNu PurANam (Namastasmai namas tasmai--VishNu purANam: 1.19.79)

तस्मै नमो मधुजिदङ्घ्रिसरोजतत्तव-
ज्ञानानुरागमहिमातिशयान्तशीम्ने ।
नाथाय नाथमुनयेऽत्र परत्र चापि
नित्यं यदीयचरणौ शरणं मदीयम्।२।

tasmai namō madhujidaṅghrisarōjatattava-
jñānānurāgamahimātiśayāntaśīmnē
nāthāya nāthamunayē'tra paratra cāpi
nityaṁ yadīyacaraṇau śaraṇaṁ madīyam|2|

Commentary:

Obeisance to that master NaTamuni, whose feet are my eternal refuge in the world and in the next, and who represents the farthest landmark that surpassing greatness, which consists, in the true knowledge of the lotus feet of Madhujith (i.e., VishNu) and intense love for them.

SlOkam 3

भूयो नमोऽपरिमिताच्युत भक्तितत्व-
ज्ञानामृताब्धिपरिवाहशुभैर्वचोभिः |
लोकेऽवतीर्णपरमार्थसमग्रभक्ति-
योगाय नाथमुनये यमिनां वराय|३|

bhūyō namō'parimitācyuta bhaktitattava-
jñānāmamr̥tābdhiparivāhaśubhairvacōbhiḥ |
lōkē'vatūrṇaparamārthasamagrabhakti-
yōgāya nāthamunayē yaminām̐ varāya|3|

Commentary:

Obeisance again to NaTamuni, the best among those who have subdued the senses, by whose holy precepts, which are the overflow of the boundless nectar-ocean of love and true knowledge of Achyuta, the true Bhakti Yoga in its entirety has descended on the earth. **The two words "ParamArTa and Samagra" are used as VisheshanNam for the Bhakthi Yogam of NaaTa Muni by AaLavandhAr to indicate that NaaTa Muni's bhakthi is svayam PrayOjanam and the means for attaining the Lord.**

The Achyutha Sabdham used by AaLavandhAr here is to show the Lord's iron clad guarantee not to lose the Prapanna and to lift that Prapanna without fail from the mire of SamsAram. His grip is such that he will not let go or abandon the Prapanna. **AaLavandhAr concludes this slOkam with the salutation to his PrAchAryA and grandfather as: "YaminAm varAya NaaTAya MunayE Nama:"**

SlOkam 4

तत्त्वेन यश्चिदचिदीश्वरतत्स्वभाव -
भोगापवर्गतदुपायगतीरुदारः |

संदर्शयन् निरमिमीत पुराणरत्नं
तस्मै नमो मुनिवराय पराशराय ।४।

tattavēna yaścidacidīśvaratatsvabhāva -
bhōgāpavargatadupāyagatīrudāraḥ
saṁdarśayan niramimīta purāṇaratnaṁ
tasmai namō munivarāya parāśarāya |4|

Swamy Adidevananda's Translation:

Obeisance to ParasarA, chief among contemplative saints, who mercifully composed the gem of puraNAs in order to present correctly the sentient, the non-sentient and Iswara, together with their real nature, and also the Jeeva's worldly enjoyment, final beatitude, means of attaining the two, and the path taken by the Jeevaas.

Commentary:

Through the three previous slOkams, ALavandhAr saluted NaaTa Muni. Now ALavandhAr offers his salutations to Sage ParAsarA, who used VishNu PurANam to instruct us on Tatthva Thraya Jn~Anam and other visEshArTams. ParAsarar picked the essential messages of Sri Sookthis by Sage VyAsar on MahA BhAratham and recast them through His VishNu PurANam hailed as **PurANa Rathnam** because of its Vishaya Gouravam - loftiness of the content). In this slOkam, ALavandhAr hints at the topics covered by Sage ParAsarA in his PurANa Rathnam: Chith-Achit-Iswara Tath SvabhAva bhOgApavarga tadhupAya gathee: (The Tatthva Thrayams, their SvabhAvams, the bhOgams like VishayAnubhavam, SvargAnubhavam, the Moksha sukhams such as KaivalyAnubhavam and Parama PadhAnubhavam). This PurANam also includes vishaya bhOgams with blemishes (hEyams) impermanent Svarga bhOgam and insignificant Kaivalya bhOgam. One can ask as to why VishNu purANam covers these hEya and asAra vishayams. **The answer is: To understand the loftiness of Tatthva Thrayam, arTa panchakam and Moksham that are most desirable, it is important to know topics with blemishes, which act as Moksha VirOdhis.**

SlOkam 5

माता पिता युवतयस्तनया विभूतिः
सर्वं यदेव नियमेन मदन्वयानाम् ।

आद्यस्य नः कुलपतेर्वकुळाभिरामं
श्रीमत् तदङ्घ्रियुगळं प्रणमामि मूर्ध्ना ||५||

mātā pitā yuvatayastanayā vibhūtiḥ
sarvaṁ yadēva niyamēna madanvayanām |
ādyasya naḥ kulapatērvakuḷābhirāmaṁ
śrīmat tadaṅghriyugaḷaṁ praṇamāmi mūradhnā ||5||

Swamy Adidevananda's Translation:

adiyEn reverently bow down my head to the blessed feet of the originator and the first Lord (Sri NammAzhwAr) of our spiritual community, which are enchanting with the vakuLa flowers - makizhampoo (offered in worship) and which alone are eternally our all-in-all our mother, father, daughters, sons, and wealth (and everything) to every one of my communities.

Commentary:

Here, ALavandhAr offers His PraNAmams to Swamy NammAzhwAr, who blessed us with the Sri Sookthi of ThiruvAimozhi, which even loftier for our enjoyment (Parama bhOgyam), most effective redeemer form samsAram (Parama ujjeevanam) and most helpful (Parama upakAram) to cross the samsAric wasteland. Swamy NammAzhwAr and his central role after celestial AchAryAs (after VishvaksEnar), His role as Prapanna SanthAna Jana Kootasthar, His upadEsam in Yoga dasai to NaaTa Muni are being celebrated here. His eminence as the leader of Prapanna Jana Kulam is saluted as: "na: Aadhyasya kula pathE: VakuLaabhirAmam Srimath ParAnkusam (Bhagavath angri yugaLam) praNamAmi". That Swamy NammAzhwAr is recognized as everything (Sarvasvam) from one's Mother, Father, Wife, children and Isvaryam (MathA, PithAa, Yuvathaya: TanayA: VibhUthi: Sarvam) for all who went before him (ALavandhAr) and all VaishNava Paramparas going to arise after him (Madh-anvayAnam niyamEna sarvam). Here ALavandhAr chooses the word PraNamAmi over NamAmi and points out that he is placing his head at the sacred feet of AzhwAr (tadangri yugaLam moordhnAa praNamAmi). Sarvasvam: MAthA (Mother) is the one, who prayed for a sathprajA (virtuous child), carried it for ten months, went through the labour pains, disregarded the asuddhis, protected it during the infant days thru breast milk and worried about its welfare all the time. PithA: The Father who served as hitha paran and protector as a child and youth. Yuvathya: The Wife, who makes him forget both the parents through being an object of his delight as a young man. TanayA: The children, who is well meaning at youth, protector at a later age and as the one, who makes his parents cross the narakam known as Puth. VibhUthi: The lack of the Iswaryam (VibhUthi) will cause much worldly suffering. Therefore, ALavandhAr says that Swamy NammAzhwAr is His Sarvasvam. Through the first three slOkams, ALavandhAr saluted the Jn~Anam and Bhakthi of NaaTa Muni. In the fourth slokam, he saluted Sage ParAsarar as the Vaidhika SrEshtar (Thraividhya vrutthAnumathar). In this fifth slOkam, he salutes Swamy NammAzhwAr as the source of his Jn~Anam.

1.YAmunA salutes the Acharyas, who opened his spiritual eye (slOkams 1-5) and particularly his grandfather, Ranga naTha Muni.

SlOkam 6

यन्मूर्ध्नि मे श्रुतिशिरस्सु च भाति यस्मिन्
अस्मन्मनोरथपथः सकलस्समेति।
स्तोष्यामि नः कुलदनं कुलदैवतं तत्
पादारविन्दमरविन्दविलोचनस्य ॥६॥

yanmūrdhni mē śrutiśirassu ca bhāti Yasmin
asmanmanōrathapathaḥ sakalassamēti |
stōṣyāmi naḥ kuladanaṁ kuladaivataṁ tat
pādāravindamaravindavilōcanasya | |6| |

2. The sthothram proper begins in slOkam 6

Swamy Adidevananda's Translation:
I shall offer my hymn of praise to the holy feet of the lotus eyed Lord - the feet, which are the sole object of my concluding philosophy of the Vedas (Upanishads). All the currents of our thoughts converge on Him who forms the treasure and tutelary deity of our lineage.

Commentary:
Through the last five slOkams, AaLavandhAr prostrated before the three great AcAryAs (NaaTa Muni, ParAsarar and NammAzhwAr) for the growth of our sampradhAyam and now begins the eulogy of SarvEswaran. He states that the **Lord's lotus feet** are his eternal and undiminishing wealth and vows to engage in eulogizing them. He elaborates further the glory of **those feet as being on**

his head, on the head of the Upanishads and as a place where all his desires come to an end. ALavandhAr recognizes the Lord's sacred feet as his SirObhUshaNam as well as for the Upanishads. **The usage of Kula dhanam (ayathna siddham and savtha: prAptham) in this slOkam refers to UpAyam for Moksham** and Kula dhaivatham (PrApya PrApakam and AasrayaNeeyam) stands in for upEyam. Those Thiruvadis are his father, Mother, Wife, Children and Wealth (Yasmin asmann-manOraTa PaTas-sakalas-samEthi). Those lotus feet of the Lord as his Sarvasvam. The "praapyathvam, sarvAdhikatthvam, Sarva MangaLaakAram and athidhurlabhathvam" of those lotus feet of the Lord are referred to here.

SlOkam 7

तत्त्वेन यस्य महिमार्णवशीकराणुः
शक्यो न मातुमपि शर्वपितामहाद्यैः |
कर्तुं तदीय महिमस्तुतिमुद्यताय मह्यां
नमोऽस्तु कवये निरपत्रपाय||७||

tattvēna yasya mahimārṇavaśīkarāṇuḥ
śakyō na mātumapi śarvapitāmahādyaiḥ |
kartuṁ tadīya mahimastutimudyatāya mahyāṁ
namō'stu kavayē nirapatrapāya||7||

---

3. The awesome Parathvam of the Lord is hinted and the insufficiency and diffidence of the poet to tackle that profound subject of the Parathvam is indicated (slOkam 7).

Swamy Adidevananda's Translation:

Fie upon me, the impudent poet! Intent as I am to sing the praise of His ocean-like glory, a single particle of whose spray it is not possible even for Siva, Bramha and the like to measure truly.

Commentary:

In the previous slOkam, AaLavandhAr declared that he is going to eulogize the Lord's lotus feet. In this slOkam, he takes a step backward form that effort through recognition of his unfitness to engage in such a daring act that is not attempted even by MahAns with greater Jn~Anam than him. He remembers that even great ones like Bramha dEvan, Sivan fail in their attempt to capture even an iota of the Vaibhavam of the Lord in their eulogies and chides himself for the foolish endeavour. He says: out of my desire to earn the name of kavi, I dared to compose this eulogy, when I know that the qualifications needed for such an effort is way beyond me. The Lord is anantha kalyANa guNa poorNan. I am a man of meagre intellect and solpa Jn~Anam. He states that his foolishness to be laughed at and every one should salute him (mahyam nama: asthu) in a form of nindhA sthuthi. Like Arjuna in the battlefield (Visrujya Sara: SApam), ALavandhAr desists from his declared intent to praise the Lord. He is angry over his sAhasam and shamelessness to venture into eulogizing the Lord, whose limitless auspicious attributes cannot become easy objects of praise.

SlOkam 8

यद्वा श्रमावधि यथामति वाऽयशक्तः
स्तैम्येवमेव खलु तेऽपि सदा स्तउवन्तः|
वेदाश्चतुर्मुखमुखाश्च महार्णवान्तः
को मज्जतोरणुकुलाचलयोर्विशेषः |८|

yadvā śramāvadhi yathāmati vā'yaśaktaḥ
staimyēvamēva khalu tē'pi sadā sta:uvantaḥ |
vēdāścaturmukhamukhāśca mahārṇavāntaḥ
kō majjatōraṇukulācalayōrviśēṣaḥ | 8 |

---

4. The sowlabhyam of the Lord is invoked to overcome the fear of tackling such a profound task (SlOkams 8-9).

Swamy Adidevananda's Translation:

Yet despite my weakness, I am justified in praising him to the limit of my capacity and to the best of my knowledge. For, verily, even the Vedas and the four-faced Bramha , ever engaged in singing his glory, could praise him only in a similar strain. What difference by contrast is there between an atom and a huge mountain range when both are submerged in the great ocean?

Commentary:

In this slOkam, the disheartened ALvandhAr, who was about to quit in his efforts to eulogize the Vaibhavam of the Lord consoles his mind and says that he will do what he can within his limits as the proper thing to do. He says to his mind: It is true that I cannot find the boundary of the Lord's kalyANa guNams and eulogize him properly. I am an asakthan (powerless one) and yet I am not going to desist from eulogizing Him. There is no rule that only those who fully comprehend the auspicious attributes of the Lord alone can eulogize Him. It is acceptable to eulogize the Lord within the limits of one's Jn~Anam and saamarTyam. Hence, I am going to eulogize Him instead of backing off. VedAs and the DevAs are always singing His praise (Sadhaapi sthuvantha: tE VedA:). Bramha dEvan might praise His Lord a little better than me (Chatur Mukha mukhaasccha yEvam yEva khalu). Anticipating protests over his sAhasam in dragging a Maha Jn~Ani, the Chathurmuka Bramha for comparison, ALavandhAr advances his reasons for such an analysis: kO majjatho: aNu kulAchalayOr visEsha: An atomic sized thing and a mountain may be both immersed in the ocean. Both have huge differences in size. When they are immersed in the deep ocean, one cannot tell their differences from outside. Similarly, my ukthis (utterances) and Bramha 's ukthis are like an atom and a mountain. Both of them however will disappear into nothingness, when compared to the vastness of the guNams of the Lord, the KalyAna guNa PoorNan (anavadhikātiśaya asankhyEya KalyANa guNa gaNa arvaNan). ALavandhAr comforts himself with the statements of Poygai AzhwAr (avar avar thaam thaam aRinthavARu yEtthi) and Swamy NammAzhwAr (tankaL anbar tamathu soll valatthAl talai talai siRanthu poosippa). They went ahead and eulogized according to the limits of their Jn~Anam and sakthi. Therefore, I am going to eulogize my Lord to my limits. He comforts his mind and says that there is no apachAram from such an endeavour. In the previous slOkam, ALavandhAr used the words: "na sakhya:" In this slOkam, he chooses the word: "sthoumi" and begins the Sthuthi. Instead of using "sthOshyAmi" to indicate the future plans, ALavandhAr uses "sthoumi " to show that he has started his eulogy (present tense).

SlOkam 9

किं चैप शक्त्यतिशयन नतेऽनुकम्प्यः
स्तोताऽपि तु स्तुति कृतेन परिश्रमेण।
तत्र श्रमस्तु सुलभो मम मन्दभुध्देः
इत्युद्यमोऽयमुचितो मम चाब्जनेत्र।९।

kiṁ caipa śaktyatiśēyana natē'nukampyaḥ
stōtā'pi tu stuti kṛtēna pariśramēṇa|
tatra śramastu sulabhō mama mandabhudhdēḥ
ityudyamō'yamucitō mama cābjanētra|9|

Swamy Adidevananda's Translation:

Moreover, this psalmist deserves to be pitied by You, not for an excellence of poetical gifts, but for his great exertion in praising You. And exertion for the purpose is quite natural to me, who am dull-witted. Oh Lotus-eyed one! This toil of mine is nonetheless meaningful, for, I can rest on Your gracious compassion which will surely be excited by this task which is beyond my capacity.

Commentary:

ALavandhAr introduces himself as "Yesha: sthOthaa" instead of saying aham sthOthaa. This is the Sanskrit protocol (MaryAdhai) to show respect for the humble poet attempting to eulogize the mighty Lord. Next, ALavandhAr moves away from the statement that he did not have the fitness to praise the Lord compared to great ones like Bramha a et al. While admitting that unfitness as a reality, he states that he is more qualified than those superior intellects for a different reason. You will see my exertions and will take pity on the strivings of mine as a dim-witted being. Your intrinsic (SvabhAveeka) Dayaa guNam will propel you to take note of my dhainyam (helplessness). You will know that I do not have the skills and cleverness (saamarTyam) to be a superior poet to tackle the mighty task at hand. I will flounder around in my efforts and will be exhausted easily (sulabha Sramam). It would be easy for you to take note of my dhainyam. I will immediately become the object of Your Dayaa. I am a mandha buddhi and do not have the tenacity and endurance like Bramha Devan to persist in my sthuthi. Therefore, your Dayaa should be the path for me to continue with my sthuthi. "Mama cha ayam udhyama: uchitha:" (This effort of mine is very appropriate for me also in the context of Paasura Vaakyam: Your anugraham will be the cause for my effort (anugraha hEthu). You will make it possible for me to complete my effort without obstacles (avignam). Like the prayer of VishNu PurANam (VP) asking for the Lord to cast His lotus soft glances on him, ALavandhAr feels emboldened to engage in the effort to eulogize the Lord: "avalOkana dhAnEnabhuyO maamm paalaya Achyutha" (VP: 1.20.16). Being Nithya sooris with superior Jn~Anam, they praise you "tath viprAsO vipanyavO jaagruvAmsas-samindhathE" /Rig Vedam1.2.7). At VishNu's Parama Padham (Yath VishNO; Paramam Padham), these mEdhAvis (Nithya Sooris) eulogize effortlessly without tiring. As for myself, the Mandha Buddhi, I too eulogize You empowered by Your karuNaa KatAksham falling on me through your anugraham to this dheenan and mandha mathi.

SlOkam 10

नावेक्षसे यदि ततो भुवनान्यमूनि
नालं प्रभो! वितुमेव कुतः प्रवृत्तिः|
एवं निसर्गसुहृति त्वयि सर्वजन्तोः
स्वामिन् न चित्रमिदमाश्रित वत्सलत्वम् ||१० ||

nāvēkṣasē yadi tatō bhuvanānyamūni
nālaṁ prabhō! vitumēva kutaḥ pravṛttiḥ|
ēvaṁ nisargasuhṛti tvayi sarvajantōḥ
svāmin na citramidamāśrita vatsalatvam ||10 ||

Swamy Adidevananda's Translation:

Oh Lord! If You do not cast your glance at these worlds, they cannot have even the power to exist; much less can they have any further development. It is not therefore strange that You, Oh Lord! Who is the natural friend of all creatures, cherish those who have sought shelter in You.

Commentary:
Once ALavandhAr addressed the Lord as Abhja nEthra in the previous slOkam, Lord's Dayaa GuNam overflowed and He cast His merciful glances on ALavandhaAr. ALavandhAr responded to the glances of the Lord with lotus eyes this way: "Oh PundareekAksha! Your anugraham does not surprise me. During the time of PraLayam, when the Aathma Vargams were powerless like the birds with broken wings, you brought them out of their misery and gave them names and form. You are my creator too and You looked at me today in that context. Hence, it does not surprise me. Upanishad declares that the Lord cast His merciful glances at the Aathma Vargams (Tath Eikshatha --Bahu syAm PrajAyEyEthi). Following the Upanishadic word, "Eikshatha., ALavandhAr chooses the word "avEkshsE" to record the Lord's lotus eyes falling on him. If

You, my Lord as anugraha visisshtan did not cast Your merciful glances, there would have been no shrushti (creation). If your sankalpam was the cause for creation (Utpatti), the created beings (uthpannaas) could not exist and move about. If You brought the Aathma Vargams from their dormant state and blessed them to go about their pravrutthi vyApArams through Your nirhEthuka krupaa, it does not surprise me that you propelled me to engage in eulogizing You. Such is the power of Your lotus eyes! I have taken refuge in You as Aaasrithan. Your anugraha visEsham is due to tour Vaathsalyam preethi VisEsham) to me. Your sankalpam is blended with Your anugraham in a tight way. You are Utpatti kaaraNan and hence You have the duties of being Rakshikkum SaraNyan (Protector of those who seek Your rakshaNam). All the creation (Sakala utpatti) and the Pravrutthi (existence and VyApAram) of those created beings are entirely due to the power of Your anugraha sankalpam. After convincing himself as a qualified one to eulogize the Lord due to His anugraha visEsham, from this slOkam onwards until the next five slOkams AlavandhAr celebrates the limb of Bhagavath Parathvam (Supremacy of the Lord over all Devaas), namely, the Lord's unique role as Moksha Dhaayakan. No other God has the power to grant Moksham. In this slOkam, ALavandhAr uses gathi SaamAnya NyAyam to establish the Lord's Parathvam (Supremacy) as natural cause behind Jagath KaaraNathvam.

SlOkam 11

स्वाभाविकानवधिकातिशयेशितृत्वं
नारायण! त्वयि न मृष्यति वैदिकः कः |
ब्रह्मा शिवः शतमखः परमः स्वराडिति
एतेऽपि यसय महिमार्णव विप्रुषस्ते|११|

svābhāvikānavadhikātiśayēśitṛtvaṁ
nārāyaṇa! tvayi na mṛṣyati vaidikaḥ kaḥ |
brahmā śivaḥ śatamakhaḥ paramaḥ svarāḍiti
ētē'pi yasaya mahimārṇava vipruṣastē|11|

Swamy Adidevananda's Translation:

Oh NaarayaNa! Who is there among the learned adherents of the Vedas that do not acknowledge Your intrinsic Godhood, endowed as You are with unsurpassable excellence? For Bramha , Siva, Indra and the supreme MuktAs are but drops in the ocean of Your glory.

कः श्रीः श्रियः परमसत्त्वशमाश्रयः कः

कः पुण्डरीकनयनः पुरुषोत्तमः कः ।

कस्यायुतायुत शतैककलांशकांशे

विश्वं विचित्रचिदचित्प्रविभागवृत्तम् ।।१२।।

kaḥ śrīḥ śriyaḥ paramasattvaśamāśrayaḥ kaḥ
kaḥ puṇḍarīkanayanaḥ puruṣōttamaḥ kaḥ |
kasyāyutāyuta śataikakalāṁśakāṁśē
viśvaṁ vicitracidacitpravibhāgavṛttam ||12||

वेदापहार गुरुपातक दैत्यपीडा-

द्यापद्विविमोचन महिष्ठफलप्रदानैः

कोऽन्यः प्रजाशुपति परिपाति कस्य

पादोदकेन स शिवः स्वशिरोधृतेन ।।१३।।

vēdāpahāra gurupātaka daityapīḍā-
dyāpadvivimōcanamahiṣṭhaphalapradānaiḥ|
kō'nyaḥ prajāśupati paripāti kasya
pādōdakēna sa śivaḥ svaśirōdhṛtēna||13|

Swamy Adidevananda's Translation:

Who else saves PrajApati and Pasupati from adversities such as deprival of the Vedas, heavy guilt and harassment by demons, and bestows upon them the greatest benefits? Who else, except You, can make Siva deserve to be called Siva (MangaLam - the auspicious one) by merely bearing on His head the water from Your feet?

कस्योदरे हरविरिञ्चमुखः प्रपञ्चः
को रक्षतीममजनिष्ट च कस्य नाभेः |
क्रान्त्वा निगीर्य पुनरुद्गिरति त्वदन्यः
कः केन वैष परवानिति शक्यशङ्कः ||१४||

kasyōdarē haraviriñcamukhaḥ prapañcaḥ
kō rakṣatīmamajaniṣṭa ca kasya nābhēḥ |
krāntvā nigīrya punarudgirati tvadanyaḥ
kaḥ kēna vaiṣa paravāniti śakyaśaṅkaḥ ||14||

Swamy Adidevananda's Translation:

In whose stomach does the Universe headed by Hara and Virincha rest? Who protects it? From whose navel has it sprung up? Who else but You, striding over all, absorbs the Universe and projects it again? And who is thee that can, even as a matter of doubt, be said to exist as Your superior?

त्वां शीलरूपचरितैः परमप्रकृष्ट-
सत्त्वेन सात्त्विकतया प्रबलैश्च शास्त्रैः |
प्रख्यातदैवपरमार्थविदां मतैश्च
नैवासुरप्रकृतयः प्रभवन्ति बोद्धुम्||१५||

tvāṁ śīlarūpacaritaiḥ paramaprakṛṣṭa-
sattvēna sāttavikatayā prabalaiśca śāstraiḥ
prakhyātadaivaparamārthavidāṁ mataiśca
naivāsuraprakṛtayaḥ prabhavanti bōddhum||15||

Swamy Adidevananda's Translation:

Those of demoniac nature are not able to recognize You by Your easily accessible disposition, loveliness of form and divine deeds -by Your supremely excellent sattvic nature; by the scriptures authoritative on account of their being sattvic in character, and by the precepts of the famous knowers of the supreme truth.

उल्लङ्घित त्रिविधसीमसमातिशायि -
संभावनं तव परिब्रढिमस्वभावं।
मायाबलेन भवताऽपि निगूह्यमानं
पश्यन्ति केचिदनिशं त्वदनन्यभावाः।।१६।।

ullaṅghita trividhasīmasamātiśāyi -
sambhāvanaṃ tava paribraḍhimasvabhāvaṃ|
māyābalēna bhavatā'pi nigūhyamānaṃ
paśyanti kēcidaniśaṃ tvadananyabhāvāḥ||16||

Swamy Adidevananda's Translation:

Some, who are inseparably united with You in thought and feeling, perceive and realize Your sovereign nature, which transcend considerations of the threefold limits (of time, space, and causation) and of another one equal or superior to them and which by the power of Maya is kept mysterious by Yourself.

यदण्डमन्डान्ततरगोचरं चयत्-
दशोत्तराण्यावरणाणि यानि च ।
गुणाः प्रधानं पुरुषः परं पदं
परात्परं ब्रह्म चते विभूतयः ।।१७।।

Yadandamandāntataragocaram cayat-
Daśottarāṇyāvaraṇāṇi yāni ca |
Guṇāh pradhānam puruṣah param padam
Parātparam Bramha cate vibhūtayah ||17||

Swamy Adidevananda's Translation:

The cosmic sphere, all that is within it, its enclosures which are more than ten, the three GuNaas, the prakriti, the individual self, the supreme abode (SrI Vaikuntam) and the Bramha n (Dhivya Mangala vigraham in the present context) who is higher than the individual self - all these are manifestations of Your splendour

वशी वदान्यो गुणवान् ऋजुः सुचिः
मृदुर्दयालुर्मधुरः स्थिरः समः।
कृती कृतज्ञस्त्वमसि स्भावतः
समस्तकल्याणगुणामृतोदधिः ॥१८॥

Vaśīvadānyo guṇavān ṛjuḥ suciḥ
Mṛdurdayālur madhuraḥ sthiraḥ samaḥ
Kṛtīkṛtajñastvamasi sbhāvataḥ
Samastakalyāṇaguṇāmṛtodadhiḥ ॥१८॥

Swamy Adidevananda's Translation:

You are, by Your own nature, submissive to the will of those that take refuge in You, bountiful, graciously accommodating to the inferior, guileless, and reliable, pure, tender, merciful, blissful, firm, free from all self-regarding duties, ever mindful of the services of the devotees and a nectar-ocean of all auspicious attributes.

उपर्युपर्यब्जाभुवोऽपि पुरुषान्
प्रकल्प्य ते ये शतमित्यनुक्रमात् ।
गिरस्वदेकैक गुणावधीप्सया
सदा स्थिता नोद्यमतो ऽतिशेरते ॥१९॥

uparyuparyabjābhuvō'pi puruṣān
prakalpya tē yē śatamityanukramāt |
girasvadēkaika guṇāvadhīpsayā
sadā sthitā nōdyamatō 'tiśēratē ॥19॥

Swamy Adidevananda's Translation:

The eternal Vedic texts which are ever eager to find out the limit of each of Your attributes (beginning with Ananda) by describing in ascending order the bliss of being higher than the lotus born Bramha Himself with the words, 'one hundred such units of bliss etc., do not, despite their incessant endeavour, go beyond the first attribute Ananda itself, it being infinite and above all enumeration

त्वदाश्रितानां जगदुद्भवस्थिति
प्रणाश संसार विमोचनादयः।
भवन्ति लीला विधयश्च वैदिकाः
तवदीयगम्भीर मनोऽनुसारिणः ।।२०।।

tvadāśritānāṁ jagadudbhavasthiti
praṇāśa saṁsāra vimōcanādayaḥ.
bhavanti līlā vidhayaśca vaidikāh
tavadīyagambhīra manō'nusāriṇaḥ ।।२०।।

Swamy Adidevananda's Translation:

The creation, sustentation and dissolution of the Universe as also release from the transmigratory existence, all of which constitute Your play, and the Vedic injunctions, which are in accord with Your profound will - all these are for the benefit of those who take shelter in You.

नमो नमो वाङ्मनसाति भूमये
नमो नमो वाङ्मनसैक भूमये।
नमो नमोऽनन्त महाविभूतये
नमो नमोऽनन्तदयैकसिन्धवे ।।२१।।

namō namō vāṅmamanasāti bhūmayē
namō namō vāṅmanasaika bhūmayē.
namō namō'nanta mahāvibhūtayē
namō namō'nantadayaikasindhavē ।।२१।।

Swamy Adidevananda's Translation:

Obeisance again and again to You who are beyond the reach of speech (Vaak) and mind; obeisance again and again to You who are the sole object of speech and mind; obeisance again and again to You of infinite great powers; obeisance again and again to You, the one ocean of infinite mercy.

---

5. Elaboration of the NaarAyana Sabdhaartham (SlOkams 10-21).

न धर्मनिषठोऽस्मि न चात्मवेदि
न भक्तिमान् त्वच्चरणारविन्दे।
अकिञ्चनोऽनन्यगतिः शरण्य!
तवत्पादमूलं शरणं प्रपद्ये ।।२२।।

na dharmaniṣaṭhō'smi na cātmavēdi
na bhaktimān tvaccaraṇāravindē.
akiñcanō'nanyagatih śaranya!
tavatpādamūlaṁ śaraṇaṁ prapadyē ||22||

---

6. The Observance of Prapatthi (NyAsA) (slOkam 22).

Swamy Adidevananda's Translation:

Oh, you worthy of being sought as refuge! I am not one established in Dharma, nor am I a knower of the self. I have no fervent devotion to Your Lotus-feet. Utterly destitute as I am, and having none else for resort, I take refuge under Your feet. (SaraNAgati)

न निन्दितं कर्म तदस्ति लोके
सहस्रशो यन्न मया व्यधायि।
सोऽहं विपाकावसरे मुकुन्द!
क्रन्दामि संप्रय्तगतिस्तवाग्रे।।२३।।

na ninditaṁ karma tadasti lōkē
sahasrasō yanna mayā vyadhāyi.
sō'haṁ vipākāvasarē mukunda!
krandāmi saṁpraytagatistavāgrē ||23||

106

Swamy Adidevananda's Translation:

There is not a single despicable deed in the world that has not been committed by me thousands of times. Oh Mukunda! Now, when those deeds are fructifying, I, the very same person, am crying out helplessly before You.

निमज्जतोऽनन्त भवार्नवान्तः
चिराय मे कूलमिवासि लब्दः।
त्वयाऽपि लब्दं भगवन्निदानीम्
अनुत्तमं पात्रमिदं दयआयआः।।२४।।

nimajjatō'nanta bhavārnavāntaḥ
cirāya mē kūlamivāsi labdaḥ.
tvayā'pi labdaṁ bhagavannidānīm
anuttamaṁ pātramidaṁ dayaāyaāḥ ।।24।।

Swamy Adidevananda's Translation:

Oh Ananta! I am getting drowned in the great ocean of transmigratory existence. At last, in You I have found the shore of that endless ocean, and You Oh Lord, have obtained now this worthiest recipient for Your mercy.

अभूतपूर्वं मम भावि किं वा
सर्वं सहे मे सहजं हि दुःखम्।
किं तु त्वदग्रे शरणागतानां
पराभवो नाथ! न तेऽनुरूपः।।२५।।

abhūtapūrvaṁ mama bhāvi kiṁ vā
sarvaṁ sahē mē sahajaṁ hi duḥkham.
kiṁ tu tvadagrē śaranāgatānāṁ
parābhavō nātha! na tē'nurūpaḥ ।।25।।

Swamy Adidevananda's Translation:

What (misery) can possibly happen to me that has not already befallen? I have been bearing everything; for misery and I have been born together. But, Oh Master! It is not becoming of You that one who has taken shelter at your feet should get frustrated in his attempt to overcome the miseries of transmigratory existence.

निरासकस्यापि न तावदुत्सहे
महेश हातुं तव पादपङ्कजम्।
रुषा निरस्तोऽपि शिशुः स्तनन्धयो
न जातु मातुश्चरणौ जिहासति॥२६॥

nirāsakasyāpi na tāvadutsahē
mahēśa hātuṁ tava pādapaṅkajam.
ruṣā nirastō'pi śiśuḥ stanandhayō
na jātu mātuścaraṇau jihāsati ||26||

Swamy Adidevananda's Translation:

Oh, Supreme Being! Even if You drive me away, I cannot relinquish Your Lotus-feet; a suckling does not at all desire to leave its mother's feet at any time, even if it has been set aside by her in anger.

तवामृतस्यन्दिनि पादपङ्कजे
निवेशितात्मा कदमन्यदिच्छति।
स्थितेऽरविन्दे मकरन्दनिर्भरे
मधुव्रतो नेक्षुरकं हि वीक्षते॥२७॥

tavāmṛtasyandini pādapaṅkajē
nivēśitātmā kadamanyadicchati.
sthitē'ravindē makarandanirbharē
madhuvratō nēkṣurakaṁ hi vīkṣatē ||27||

Swamy Adidevananda's Translation:

How can my mind, which is firmly set upon Your Lotus-feet shedding nectar, ever be desirous of anything else? As is well known, when there exists a lotus laden with honey nearby, a bee does not even glance at the Ikshuraka flower (NeermuLLi - thorny flower without fragrance or honey).

7. Declaration of his appropriateness (SvayogyA Kathanam /adhikAram) by YaamunA for the performance of his Prapatthi (slOkams 23-27).

त्वदङ्घ्रिमुद्दिश्य कदाऽपिकेनचित्
यथा तथा वाऽपि सकृत् कृतोऽञ्जलिः।
तदैव मुष्नात्यशुभाण्यशेषतः
शुभाणि पुष्णाति न जातु हीयते।।२८।।

tvadaṅghrimuddiśya kadā'pikēnacit
yathā tathā vā'pi sakṛt kṛtō'ñjaliḥ.
tadaiva muṣnātyaśubhānyaśēṣataḥ
śubhāṇi puṣṇāti na jātu hīyatē |28||

Swamy Adidevananda's Translation:

Whosoever, in whatever manner, at whatever time, supplicates to You with palms joined even once, that act dispels at once all his miseries and contributes to his well-being. An act of supplication to You is never in vain

उदीर्णसंसारदवाशुशुक्षणिम्
क्षणेन निर्वाप्य परां च निर्वृतिम्।
प्रयच्छति त्वच्चरणारुणाम्भुज-
द्वयानुरागामृतशिन्धुशीकरः।।२९।।

udīrṇasaṁsāradavāśuśukṣaṇim
 kṣaṇēna nirvāpya parāṁ ca nirvṛtim.
pravacchati tvaccaraṇāruṇāmbhuj
dvayānurāgāmṛtaśindhuśīkaraḥ ||29||

109

Swamy Adidevananda's Translation:

A drop from the nectar-ocean of love to Your lovely Lotus-feet extinguishes the blazing forest conflagration of transmigratory existence in an instant and bestows supreme bliss.

Statement of the fact that the simple-to-perform Prapatthi has disproportionately large dividends (slOkams 28-29).

विलासविक्रान्त परावरालयं
नमस्यदार्तिक्षपणे कृतक्षणम्।
धनं मदीयं तव पाद पङ्कजं
कदा नु साक्षात्करवाणि चक्षुषा।।३०।।

Swamy Adidevananda's Translation:

vilāsavikrānta parāvarālayaṁ
namasyadārtikṣapaṇē kr̥takṣaṇam.
dhanaṁ madīyaṁ tava pāda paṅkajaṁ
kadā nu sākṣātkaravāṇi cakṣuṣā. ।।30।।

Oh Trivikrama! When will Your Lotus-feet, bearing the marks of conch, discus, the wish-
granting heavenly tree, banner, lotus, hook (ankusam) and thunderbolt (VajrAyudham), adorn
my head?

विराजमानोज्ज्वल पीतवाससं
स्मितातसीसून समामलच्छविम्।
निमग्ननाभिं तनुमध्यमुन्नतं
विशाल वक्षस्स्थल शोभिलक्षणम्।।३२।।

virājamānōjjvala pītavāsasaṁ
smitātasīsūna samāmalacchavim.

nimagnanābhim tanumadhyamunnatam
visāla vakṣassthala śōbhilakṣaṇam ||32||

Swamy Adidevananda's Translation:

Who is beautifully clad in shining yellow raiment (Peethaambharam), whose pure splendour is
equal to that of a blooming kaayaampoo (a dark blue hued flower), who is endowed with a
depressed navel, slender waist, high stature and the shining (Srivatsam) mark on the broad chest.
The slOkaas 33 to 40 have the following in its essence:
1. The description of the Divine form of Lord NaarayaNaa in absolute and relative terms
i.e., the form in some slOkaas reference is made to the form through similes like blooming lotus, the moon and through Sri Lakshmi Herself.
2. An introduction to Sri Lakshmi and Her transcendental qualities befitting our Lord and
a reference to Sri Vaikuntam itself through Sri Adisesha along with his mod of service
to the Lord.

चकासतं ज्याकिकिणकर्कशैः शुभैः
चतुर्भिराजानु विलम्बिभिर्भुजैः।
प्रियावतंसोत्पलकर्णभूषण-
श्रथालकाबन्धविमर्दशंसिभिः॥३३॥

cakāsatam jyākikiṇakarkaśaiḥ śubhaiḥ
caturbhirājānu vilambibhirbhujaiḥ.
priyāvatamsōtpalakarnabhūsana-
ślathālakābandhavimardaśamsibhiḥ ||33||

Swamy Adidevananda's Translation:

Who shines with four auspicious arms which reach the knees, and have the rough scars of the
bowstring, and which speak of their contact with the crest-lily, the ear-ornament and the loose
curls of the braid of Your beloved.

उदग्रपीनांस विलम्बिकुण्डला -
लकावली बन्धुर कम्बुकन्धरम्।
मुखश्रिया न्यक्कृत पूर्ण निर्मला-
मृतांशुबिम्बाम्बुरुहोज्ज्वलश्रियम्।।३४।।

udagrapīnāṁsa vilambikuṇḍalā -
lakāvalī bandhura kambukandharam.
mukhaśriyā nyakkṛta pūrṇa nirmalā-
mṛtāṁśubimbāmburuhōjjvalaśriyam. ||34||

Swamy Adidevananda's Translation:

Whose conch like neck is adorned with curls of hair and earrings hanging over the high and large
shoulders, and by the lustrous beauty of whose face the brilliant splendor of the spotless Moon
and the blooming lotus are put to shame.

प्रबुत्त मुक्ताम्बुजचारुलोचनं

सविभ्रम भ्रूलतं उज्जवलाधरम्।

शुचिस्मितं कोमलगण्डं उन्नसं

ललाट पर्यन्तविलम्बितालकम्।।३५।।

prabutta mukttāmbujacārulocanaṁ
savibhrama bhrūlataṁ ujjavalādharam.
śucismitaṁ komalagaṇḍaṁ unnasaṁ
lalāṭa paryantavilambitālakam ||35||

Swamy Adidevananda's Translation:

Who has eyes charming like the petals of a fresh and full-blown lotus, gracious creep like brows, shining lips, pleasant smile, soft cheeks, prominent nose, and curls hanging up to the forehead.

स्फुरत्किरीटाङ्गद हार कण्ठिका-

मणीन्द्र काञ्ची गुण नूपुरादिभिः।

रथाङ्ग शङ्खासि गदा धनुवरैः

लसत्तुलस्या वनमालयोज्जवलम्।।३६।।

sphuratkirīṭāṅgada hāra kaṇṭhikā-
maṇīndra kāñcī guṇa nūpurādibhiḥ.
rathāṅga śaṅkhāsi gadā dhanuvaraiḥ
lasattulasyā vanamālayojjavalam ||36||

Swamy Adidevananda's Translation:

Who is handsome with a shining diadem (kreedam), bracelets (thOLvaLai), garland of pearls, necklace, the kaustubha gem, waistband, anklets etc. and with the divine discus, conch, sword, mace, the divine excellent bow and the most beautiful, soft fragrant tuLasi garland.

चकर्थ यस्या भवनं भुजान्तरं

तव प्रियं धाम यदीय जन्मभूः।

जगत्समस्तं यदपाङ्गसंश्रयं

यदर्थमम्भोधिरमन्थ्यबन्धि च।।३७।।

cakartha yasyā bhavanaṃ bhujāntaram
tava priyaṃ dhāma yadīya janmabhūḥ.
jagatsamastaṃ yadapāṅgasaṃśrayam
yadarthamambhodhiramanthyabandhi ca ||37||

Swamy Adidevananda's Translation:

Who has made his chest the abode of SrI, whose birthplace is Your beloved abode (the milky Ocean), in whose side glance the entire Universe takes refuge and for whose sake the ocean was churned and causewayed.

स्ववैश्वरूप्येण सदाऽनुभूतयाऽपि

अपूर्वं वाद्विस्मयमादधानया।

गुणेन रूपेण विलासचेष्टितैः

सदा तवैवोचितया तव श्रिया।।३८।।

svavaiśvarūpyeṇa sadā'nubhūtayā'pi
apūrva vādvismayamādadhānayā.
guṇena rūpeṇa vilāsacoṣṭitaiḥ
sadā tavaivocitayā tava śriyā ||38||

तया सहासीनंमनन्तभोगिनि

प्रकृष्ट विज्ञानबलैकधामनि

फणामणिव्रातमयूखमण्डल-

प्रकाशमानोदरदिव्यधामनि।।३९।।

tayā sahāsīnammanantabhogini
prakṛṣṭa viñjānabalaikadhāmani
phaṇāmaṇivrātamayūkhamaṇḍala-
prakāśamānodaradivyadhāmani ||39||

निवासशय्यासनपादुकांशुको-

पधान वर्षातपवारणादिभिः।

शरीरभेदैस्तव शेषतां गतैः

यथोचितं शेष इतीरिते जनैः।।४०।।

nivāsaśayyāsanapādukāṃśuko-
padhāna varṣātapavāraṇādibhiḥ.

śarīrabhedaistava śeṣatāṃ gataiḥ

yathocitaṃ śeṣa itīrite janaiḥ ||40||

Swamy Adidevananda's Translation for Slokams 38 to 40:

Who is seated with tat SrI (MahA LakshmI), who by Her attribute, beauty, agreeable sports and merciful deed is ever a match for You and You alone, and who creates unprecedented delight for You (as one separate) though She is eternally comprehended in Your cosmic form on the Divine ThiruvananthAzhwAn (AdhisEshan), who is the sole seat of excellent knowledge and strength, within the divine abode (Sri Vaikuntam) the inside of which is illuminated by the circle of rays emanating from the clustered gems of his hoods, and who is aptly designated by devotees as sesha on account of the different forms he has assumed for serving You such as residence, couch, seat, sandals, raiments (pEthAmbaram), pillow and shelter from sun and rain

दासस्सखा वाहनमासनं ध्वजो

यस्ते वितानं व्यजनं त्रयीमययः।

उपस्थितं तेन पुरो गरुत्मता

त्वदङ्घिसम्मर्दकिणाङ्क शोभिणा॥४१॥

dāsassakhā vāhanamāsanaṃ dhvajo
yaste vitānaṃ vyajanaṃ trayīmayayaḥ.
upasthitaṃ tena puro garutmatā
tvadaṅghisammardakiṇāṅka śobhiṇā ||41||

Swamy Adidevananda's Translation:

Having at hand for Your service Garutman who isYour servant, fiend, vehicle, seat, banner, canopy and fan, and whose form is mad up of the three Vedas, and who is beautiful with the scar-sign due to the contact of Your feet. Swamy Adidevananda comments SlOkaas 41 and 42 further introduces eternal souls like Vainatheya (Peria Thiruvadi - Garudaaazhwan) and Vishvaksenar with their modes of service to our Lord and the uniqueness of these Nithysoories as a result of close contact (saamipya).

त्वदीय भुक्तोज्झित शेषभोजिना

त्वया निसृष्टात्मभरेण यद्यथा।

प्रियेण सेनापतिना न्यवेदि तत्

तथाऽनुजानन्तमुदारवीक्षणैः ।।४२।।

tvadīya bhuktojjhita śeṣabhojinā
tvayā nisṛṣṭātmabhareṇa yadyathā.
priyeṇa senāpatinā nyavedi tat
tathā'nujānantamudāravīkṣaṇaiḥ ।।42।।

Swamy Adidevananda's translation:

Who approves with noble glance whatever communication is brought to You by your beloved chief of hosts (VishvaksEnar), who partakes of the remnants of Your food, and on whom has been bestowed the charge (of Your sovereignty).

SlOkam 43:
 SlOkam 43 brings out the supreme qualities of other nitya sooris and mukta AtmAs in their pure state devoid of egoism and material infatuations etc. and thereby glorifying the Lord as His unique attributes. This slOkam also highlights the reality of the Jeeva as a sesha to the Lord, who is the Seshi and the enjoyment of the jeeva in complete service of the Lord in SAmipya (being aware or being near to Lord NaarayaNa).

Who is served by the eternal ones suited to You on account of their being possessing the attributes of omniscience etc, the eternal ones, who are free from all the impurities of afflictions (such as nascence, egoism etc.), whose sole delight consists in being spontaneously devoted to Your service, and who constantly wait upon You with appropriate service.

हताखिल क्लेशमलैः स्भावतः

त्वदानुकूलयैकरसैस्तवोचितैः।

गहीततत्तत्परिचार साधनैः

निषेव्यमाणं सचिवैर्यथोचितम्।।४३।।

hatākhila kleśamalaiḥ sbhāvataḥ
tvadānukūlayaikarasaistavocitaiḥ.
gahītatattatparicāra sādhanaiḥ
niṣevyamāṇaṃ sacivairyathocitam || 43 ||

Swamy Adidevananda's translation:

Who, of long arms, exhilarates Your queen (SrI MahA LakshmI) with lovely and skilful sports which consists of diverse new sentiments and emotions, and which make time measured as eons (yugas and yugas) and so forth appear as a fraction of second.

अपूर्व नानारसभाव निर्भर-

प्रबद्ध्या मुग्ध विदग्धलीलया।

क्षणाणुवत् क्षिसपरादिकालया

प्रहर्षयन्तं महिषीं महाभुजम्।।४४।।

apūrva nānārasabhāva nirbhara-
prabaddhyā mugdha vidagdhalīlayā.
kṣaṇāṇuvat kṣiptaparādikālayā
praharṣayantaṃ mahiṣīṃ mahābhujam ।। 44 ।।

Swamy Adidevananda's translation: 44

Who, of long arms, exhilarates Your queen (SrI MahA LakshmI) with lovely and skilful sports which consists of diverse new sentiments and emotions, and which make time measured as eons (yugas and yugas) and so forth appear as a fraction of second

अचिन्त्य दिव्याद्भुत नित्य यैवन-

स्वभावलावण्य मयामृतोदधिम्।

श्रियः श्रियं भक्त जनैक जीवितमं

समर्थमापत्सखंमर्थिकल्पकम्।।४५।।

acintya divyādbhuta nitya yaivana-
svabhāvalāvaṇya mayāmṛtodadhim.
śriyaḥ śriyaṃ bhakta janaika jīvitamaṃ
samarthamāpatsakhaṃmarthikalpakam।।45।।

Meaning according to Sri V. Madhava Kannan:(SlOkA-45)

Incomprehensible, unperceivable, transcendental, most wonderful, eternal, naturally ever Youthful, blue hued nectarine form of Divine Bodied Lord- the One who is the SrI of SrI Mahalakshmi (wealth of Sri Mahalakshmi); who is the very life breadth of His dearest devotes; Most Omniscient, Omnipotent, full of power; Shakthimaan; Sarva Shakthan; who helps (us) in danger (friend in need);

who grants everything whatever asked for by His devotees like the kalpaka vruksham.

भवन्तमेवानुचरन् निरन्तरं

प्रशान्त निश्शेषमनोरथान्तरः।

कदाऽहमैकान्तिक नित्यकिङ्करः

प्रहरषयिष्यामि सनाथ जीवितः।।४६।।

bhavantamevānucaran nirantaraṃ
praśānta niśśeṣamanorathāntaraḥ.
kadā'hamaikāntika nityakiṅkaraḥ
praharaṣayiṣyāmi sanātha jīvitaḥ ||46||

Swamy Adidevananda's translation:

Constantly waiting on You alone, with all other desires absolutely quenched, when shall I, an eternal servant of You and You alone, delight You, having You as the Lord of my life

9. Revelation of the meaning of the uttara KanTam of Dhvayam as that which deals with the fruit of the Prapatthi (slOkams 30-46).

धिगशुचिमविनीतं निर्भयं (निर्दयं) मामलज्जं

परम पुरुष योऽहं योगिवर्यांग्रण्यैः।

विधिशिव सनकाद्यैध्यातुमत्यन्त दूरं

तव परिजनभावं कामये कामवृत्तः।।४७।।

dhigaśucimavinītaṃ nirbhayaṃ (nirdayaṃ) māmalajjaṃ
parama puruṣa yo'haṃ yogivaryāgraṇyaiḥ.
vidhiśiva sanakādyaidhyātumatyanta dūraṃ
tava parijanabhāvaṃ kāmaye kāmavṛttaḥ ||47||

Swamy Adidevananda's translation:

Oh, Supreme Purusha! Fie upon me who am impure, immodest, audacious, impudent and self-willed and yet desirous of the rank of Your servant, which even those worthy of being counted foremost among the supreme yOgins, Bramha, Siva and Sanaka cannot conceive in their minds.

---

10. Expression of his regret over hitherto wasted days due to his lack of intensity to pursue the fruits of Prapatthi thru the observance of the appropriate Upaayam (Nirvedam over his missed opportunities. slOkam 47).

अपराध सहस्र भाजनं
पतितं भीमभवार्णवोदरे।
अगतिंशरणागतं हरे
कपयाकेवलमात्मसात् कुरु।।४८।।

aparādha sahasra bhājanaṁ
patitaṁ bhīmabhavārṇavōdarē.
agatiṁśaraṇāgataṁ harē
kapayākēvalamātmasāt kuru ।।48।।

Swamy Adidevananda's translation:

Oh Hari! Pray, make my own out of sheer grace - me who am fallen into the depths of the terrible ocean of worldly existence, and who, being resort less, have sought refuge at Your feet.

अविवेक घनान्धदिङ्मुखे
बहुधा सन्ततुदुःखवर्षिणि।
भगवन् भवदुर्दिन पथः
स्खलितं मामवलोकयाच्युत।।४९।।

avivēka ghanāndhadiṅmukhē
bahudhā santatuduḥkhavarṣiṇi.
bhagavan bhavadurdina pathaḥ
skhalitaṁ māmavalōkayācyuta ।।49।।

Swamy Adidevananda's translation:

Oh Bhagavan, Oh Achyuta, cast Your glance on me who have swerved from the path of spiritual life on this gloomy and rainy day of worldly existence, when the quarters of the sky are darkened with the cloud of non-discrimination, which continually rains sorrows on me in various ways.

नमृषा परमार्थ मेव मे
श्रुणु विज्ञापनमेकमग्रतः।
यदि मे न मेदयिष्यसे ततो
दयनीयस्तव नाथ दुर्लभः।।५०।।

namrṣā paramārtha mēva mē
śruṇu vijñāpanamēkamagrataḥ.
yadi mē na mēdayisyasē tatō
dayanīyastava nātha durlabhaḥ ||50||

Meaning according to Sri V. Madhavakkannan:

Oh NathA! Master and Lord of NithyasUris! The sincere truthful (with no deceit or any other wrong intention) plea and prayer of mine- Please listen to that. That is: If You do not take pity on me and be merciful at me- then none would be there for You to be blessed by Your compassion at all. (There will be none)

तदहं त्वदृते न नाथवान्
मदृते त्वं दयनीय वान न च।
विधिनिर्मितमेतमन्वयं
भगवन् पालय मा स्म जीहपः।।५१।।

tadahaṁ tvadṛtē na nāthavān
madṛtē tvaṁ dayanīya vāna na ca.
vidhinirmitamētamanvayaṁ
bhagavan pālaya mā sma jīhapaḥ ||51||

Swamy Adidevananda's translation:

Therefore, without You I am lost for a Lord, and without me You are lost for a worthy recipient for Your compassion. Preserve, Oh Lord! this relation (of Your Lordship and my pitiableness), which is ordained by fate, and spurn me not.

---

11. The importance of Mahaa Viswasam on the fruits to be gained by Prapatthi (slOkams 48- 51).

वपुरादिषु योऽपि कोऽपि वा
गुणतोऽसानि यथा तथाविधः।
तदयं तव पादपद्मयोः
अहमदैव मया समर्पितः॥५२॥

vapurādiṣu yō'pi kō'pi vā
guṇatō'sāni yathā tathāvidhaḥ.
tadayaṁ tava pādapadmayōḥ
ahamadyaiva mayā samarpitaḥ||52||

Swamy Adidevananda's translation:

Whatever might be the nature of the body and the organs I am endowed with according to the GuNaas of Prakriti, I am offering them this very moment at Your Lotus-feet, as also what is denoted as "I" in me.

मम नाथ यदस्ति योऽस्म्यहं
सकलं तद्धि तवैव माधव!।
नियतस्वमिति प्रबुद्धधीः
अथवा किं नु समर्पयामि ते॥५३॥

mama nātha yadasti yō'smyahaṁ
sakalaṁ taddhi tavaiva mādhava!. |
niyatasvamiti prabuddhadhīh
athavā kiṁ nu samarpayāmi tē || 53||

Swamy Adidevananda's translation:

Oh Lord! Whatever I have, whatever I am, all these, verily, are Your own already. What then shall I offer You? Oh MadhavA! Being thus awakened to the consciousness that all these are Your own inalienable property, there is nothing left for me to offer

अवबोदित वानिमां यथा
मयि नित्यां भवदीयतां स्वयम्।
कृपयैवमनन्यभोग्यतां
भगवन्! भक्तिमपि प्रयच्छ मे।।५४।।

avabōdita vānimāṁ yathā
mayi nityāṁ bhavadīyatāṁ svayam.
kṛpayaivamananyabhōgyatāṁ
bhagavan! bhaktimapi prayaccha mē ।।54।।

Swamy Adidevananda's translation:

As You, your self has awakened in me this consciousness of being eternally Yours, so too, Oh Lord, grant me, out of compassion, that Bhakti which is of the nature of enjoying You and You alone.

तव दास्यसुखैकसङ्गिनां
भवनेष्वस्त्वपि कीटजन्म मे।
इतरावसथेषु मा स्म भूत्
अपि मे जन्म चतुर्मुखात्मना।।५५।।

tava dāsyasukhaikasaṅginām
bhavanēṣvastvapi kīṭajanma mē.
itarāvasathēsu mā sma bhūt
api mē janma caturmukhātmanā।।55।।

Swamy Adidevananda's translation:

May I be born even as a worm in the homes of those who are solely devoted to the joy of serving You; but let me not be born even as the four-faced Bramha in the abodes of those who are otherwise disposed

सकृत् त्वदाकारविलोकनाशया
तृणीकृतानुत्तमभुक्तिमुक्तिभिः।
महात्मभिर्मामवलोक्यतां नय
क्षणेऽपि तेयद्विरहोऽदिदुखःसहः।।५६।।

sakr̥t tvadākāravilōkanāśayā
tr̥ṇīkr̥tānuttamabhuktimuktibhiḥ.
mahātmabhirmāmavalōkyatāṁ naya
kṣaṇē'pi tēyadvirahō'didukhaḥsahaḥ ||56||

Swamy Adidevananda's translation:

Make me an object worthy of the benign look of great souls, who with the hope of having even a
single glance at Your form is ready to reject as worthless as a blade of grass, even the highest
enjoyments and liberation, and whose separation even for a moment is very unendurable to You

न देहं न प्राणान् न च सुखमशेषाभिलषितं
न चात्मानं नान्यत् किमपि तव शेषत्वविभवात्।
बहिर्भूतं नाथ क्षणमपि सहे यातुशतधा
विनाशं तत् सत्यं मधुमथन विज्ञापनमिदम्।।५७।।

na dēhaṁ na prāṇān na ca sukhamaśēṣābhilaṣitaṁ
na cātmānaṁ nānyat kimapi tava śēṣatvavibhavāt.
bahirbhūtaṁ nātha kṣaṇamapi sahē yātuśatadhā
vināśaṁ tat satyaṁ madhumathana vijñāpanamidam ||57||

Swamy Adidevananda's translation:

Oh Lord, neither the body, nor the praNaas, nor the happiness coveted by all, nor even the self,
nor anything else that is outside the requirements for Your service, can I, even for a moment put
up with? Let them perish in a hundred ways. This is in all truth in my entreaty to You, Oh slayer
of Madhu!

दुरन्तस्यानादेरपरिहरणीयस्य महतः
निहीनाचारोऽहं नृपशुरशुभस्यास्पदमपि।
दयासिन्धो!बन्धो!निरवदिक वात्सल्य जलदे!
तव स्मारं गुणगणमितीच्छामि गतभईः।।५८।।

durantasyānādērapariharaṇīyasya mahataḥ
nihīnācārō'haṁ nrpaśuraśubhasyāspadamapi.
dayāsindhō!bandhō!niravadika vātsalya jaladē!
tava smāraṁ guṇagaṇamitīcchāmi gatabhaiḥ ||58||

Swamy Adidevananda's translation:
Though I, a beast of a human (nrupasu) without any standard of conduct, being the seat of all vices and cruelty, am fated for an eternal and calamitous destiny, still I am free from all fear, remembering You again and again, You an ocean of Mercy (Dayaa sindho) and parental love, and innumerable virtues of a similar nature.
Even though I am a base-behaved beastly man and the abode of great, inescapable, beginningless and ominous sins, Oh Ocean of Mercy, Oh Parent, oh sea of boundless affection, freed from all fear by remembering Thy infinite attributes (kalayana guNam) again and again, I pray in the above manner

अनिच्छन्नप्येवं यदि पुनरितीच्छन्निव रजस्-
तमश्छन्नस्छद्मस्तुतिवचन भङ्गीमरचयम्।
तथाऽपित्थंरूपं वचनमवलम्ब्यापि कृपया
त्वमेवैवंभूतं धरमणीधर मे शिक्षय मनः।।५९।।

anicchannapyēvaṁ yadi punaritīcchanniva rajas-
tamaśchannaschadmastutivacana bhaṅgīmaracayam.
tathā'pitthaṁrūpaṁ vacanamavalambyāpi krpayā
tvamēvaivaṁbhūtaṁ dharamaṇīdhara mē śikṣaya manaḥ.
||59||

Meaning according to Sri V. Madhavakkannan:

Meaning according to Sri V. Madhavakkannan:

Engulfed by rajasa, thamO guNas and covered by the same; with no strong desire (perhaps) for the sEshavriithi- though spelt out in earlier verses; having desired thus now- with deceit in mind and outward asking and desiring for sEshavritthi; I am uttering this verse outwardly for the name sake. Be it so. Even then, please bless me even such a deceitful statement of mine itself as an excuse, and oh Lord! The One who mercifully and compassionately lifted the BhUmAdEvi of immense patience and helped us! With the same dayA, compassion, and ocean of mercy, please correct and transform my mind.

पिता त्वं माता त्वं प्रियसुहृत्

त्वमेव त्वं मित्रं गुरुरसि जगताम्।

त्वदीयस्त्वद्भृत्यस्तव परिजनस्त्वद्गतिरहं

प्रपन्नश्चैवं सत्यहमपि तवैवास्मि हि भरः।।६०।।

pitā tvaṁ mātā tvaṁ priyasuhṛt
tvamēva tvaṁ mitraṁ gururasi jagatām.
tvadīyastvadbhṛtyastava parijanastvadgatirahaṁ
prapannaścaivaṁ satyahamapi tavaivāsmi hi bharaḥ ||60||

Meaning according to Sri V. Madhavakkannan:
For all the worlds, you are everything; You are alone are the father; Mother; darling son; dearest friend; close relation; the Acharya who dispels the darkness of ignorance; - the end that we attain- everything is thus You and You alone. I am Your eternal servant. I need to be brought up by You (tvad brutya:); Your servant (tava parijana:); You are the end and goal for me (tvad gathi:). I am also the One who has performed SaraNAgathi at Your Lotus Feet (Prapanna ca). When such is the case, I am also the goal for You- Am I not?

जनित्वाऽहं वंशे महति जगति ख्यातयशसां

सुचीनां युक्तानां गुणपरुषतत्त्ववस्थिति विदाम्।

निसर्गादेव त्वच्चरणकमलैकान्तमनसाम्

अधोऽधः पापात्मा शरणद निमज्जामि तमसि

।।६१।।

janitvā'haṁ vaṁśē mahati jagati khyātayaśasāṁ
sucīnāṁ yuktānāṁ guṇaparuṣatattavasthiti vidām.
nisargādēva tvaccaraṇakamalaikāntamanasām
adhō'dhaḥ pāpātmā śaraṇada nimajjāmi tamasi
||61||

Meaning according to Sri V. Madhavakkannan:

I having been blessed to be born in the lineage of world's most glorious anushtAthAs (one who performs karma anushtAnams in strict and full accordance with sAsthrAs and nothing else); who are parama vaideekAas; who have performed great yaagAs and yajn~As in their lives; who have performed (karma/jn~Ana, bhakti) Yogas; who have fully comprehended the exact truths about sentient, non-sentient entities (Chith and achith tattva respectively), Supreme entity (Iswara tattva) in crystal clear manner; who have understood Purusha, Jeeva tattvam unambiguously and the eternal relation between them; who have since their births? Been devoted to only Your red Lotus Feet alone; and had the mind contemplating always only on the Lotus Feet of Yours; - am the personification of all gravest sins; and drowning myself in the darkness of thamasic world (World of ignorance) and going deeper and deeper. Oh SaraNyA! Please see me? (Bless me).

अमर्यादः क्षुद्रः चलमतिः असूयाप्रसवभूः

कृतघ्नो दुर्मानि स्मरपरवशो वञ्चनरः।

नृशंसःपापिष्ठः कथमहमितो दुःखजलधेः

अपारादुत्तीर्णस्तव परिचरेयं चरणयओः॥६२॥

amaryādaḥ kṣudraḥ calamatiḥ asūyāprasavabhūḥ
kṛtaghnō durmāni smaraparavaśō vañcanaraḥ.
nṛśaṁsahpāpisṭhaḥ kathamahamitō duḥkhajaladhēḥ
apārāduttīrṇastava paricarēyaṁ caraṇayaōḥ||62||

Meaning according to Sri V. Madhavakkannan:

Sri Alavandhar says in this slOkam that everyone- be from all caste and creed- they need to think of themselves of qualities housed in him (as listed below) - as there is none who is perfect? Except Sriya: Pathi Sriman Narayanan.

I am the epitome of all bad qualities as enlisted here: One who has crossed the bounds of

established rules, engaging in trivial /worldly /material/sensual pursuits, never steady / fickle mind (chanchalam), place where jealousy is born, ungrateful one, ill feelings towards fellow human beings, fallen into the gamut of desires and sensual impulses, skilfully deceiving others (At cheating others), engaging in violent acts and incorrigible sinner (MahA Paapi). Am falling down and immersed in Samsaaric Ocean. How? How will I be able to utter Your name even

रघुवर यदभूस्त्वं तादृशो वायसस्य

प्रणत इति दयालुर्यच्च चैद्यस्य कृष्णः।

प्रतिभव मपराद्धुर्मग्ध सायुज्यदोऽभू:
वद किमपदमागस्तस्यतेऽस्तिक्षमायाः।।६३।।

raghuvara yadabhūstvaṁ tādṛśō vāyasasya

praṇata iti dayāluryacca caidyasya kṛṣṇaḥ.

prati bhava maparāddhurmagdha sāyuj yadō'bhūḥ

vada ki mapadamāgast asyat ē'st i kṣamāyāḥ।।63।।

Meaning according to Sri V. Madhavakkannan:

Oh the zenith of Raghu vamsa! The vamsa (lineage) that was known for the protection of those who have surrendered! When the kAkAsura fell on the ground, (even in other direction) You accepted the same as if it is SaraNAgathi at Your Feet and pardoned its aparAdham then and there. You appeared as if You do not even know or realise the apachAram committed by the asurA and most compassionately condoned the Kaakaasuran. What is the reason? You are the sweetest KaNNan; and on the incorrigible SisupAlan- who was bent upon committing only apachArams on You ceaselessly, what is that You granted mOksham to him? It is all due to Your vaathsalyam and greatest compassion. For such You, what is the apachAram which is not or which cannot be condoned and pardoned by Your patience and compassion? (None).

---

14. Statement on the Lord's kAruNyam, sambhandham (Bhandhutvam) as the hope for in the context of his Prapatthi (slOkam 58-63

ननु प्रपन्नः सकलदेव नाथ

तवाहमस्मीति च याचमानः।

तवानुकमप्यःस्मरतः प्रतिज्ञां

मदेकवर्जं किमदं व्रतं ते।।६४।।

nanu prapannaḥ sakaladēva nātha
tavāhamasmīti ca yācamānaḥ.
tavānukamapyahsmarataḥ pratijñāṁ
madēkavarjaṁ kimadaṁ vrataṁ tē ।।64।।

Meaning according to Sri V. Madhavakkannan:

Raghu nAthA! My nAthA! One who has performed SaraNAgathi once with a desire to be Your servant; and pleads for the same- whoever it is; You had taken a vow, pledge (vratham) which

You would never ever forget. Isn't that Your limitless compassion? Such a sankalpam of Yours to protect all those SaraNAgatha whoever they are? Did You exclude me (when You made that sankalpam)?

15. Reminding the Lord of his saraNAgatha RakshaNa vratham of the Lord and prayer to include him in that vratham (slOkam 64).

अकृत्रिमत्वच्चरणारविन्दे-
प्रेमप्रकर्षावधिमात्मवन्तम्।
पितामहं नाथमुनिं विलोक्य
प्रसीद मद्वृत्तमचिन्तयित्वा।।६५।।

akrtrimatvaccaraṇāravindē-
prēmaprakarṣāvadhimātmavantam.
pitāmaham nāthamunim vilōkya
prasīda madvrttamacintayitvā|| 65||

Meaning according to Sri V. Madhavakkannan:

Sriman NaTamuni- my grandfather, my Acharya's Acharya- the one who has the AtmA, with
the personification and ultimate of Unalloyed natural flawless devotion and without expecting
any other fruits other than enjoyment of Your Lotus Feet; Such great Yoga purusha; - thinking
of any association with him (as his grandson as well as his shishya's Sishya), please do not look
down upon me for my pApAs and bless me with Your grace.

16. Statement on the glories of the anugraham and sambhandham of the Acharya for successful Prapatthi and inclusion of his fearlessness (Nirbhayam) as a result of performing Prapatthi, even if he does not have the qualifications of his own (naicchiyAnusandhAnam)--slOkam 65 (final slokam).

19. Bibliography

1. Purusha Suktam from श्वेताश्वतरोपनिषद्- Swetasvatara Upanishad -8- https://upanishads.org.in/upanishads/9/3/8

2. https://www.google.co.in/search?q=from+where+this+verse+is+taken+

3. Subhashitani Collections from Net.

4. N https://www.facebook.com/shdve/posts/1360622764454114

5. https://www.tititudorancea.com/z/brahmavidya_upanishad_sanskrit_devanagari

6. Selections from Minor Upanishads, translated by K. N. Aiyar, 1914 - http://oaks.nvg.org/minor-upanishads.html

7. Brahma Vidya (Chandogya Ch.8) Kindle Edition

8. Ubhaya Vedanta Grantha Mala, Srimad Bhagavad Gita, with Srimad Bhagavad Ramanuja's Bhashya, and Srimad Vedanta Desika's Tatparya Chandrika and Srimad Abhinava Desika Uttamur Viraraghavacharya's detailed Introduction and Rasavada Foot notes. Sri. Uttamur Viraraghavacharya's, centenary Trust, Chennai

9. श्रीव्यासकृत ब्रह्मसूत्राणि, by 44th Pontiff (Azagiya Singer), Sri Ahobila Matam.

10. Nava Ratna Malika, Sri Bhashyam of Sri. Ramanujar with Tamil Transliteration by Sri. U. Ve Tirumalai Caturvedi Shatakrutu Navalpakkam. V. Vasudevachariyar (Vol II, III), Vainavan Kural Publication, Chennai-78, First Publication- Vol II-2017 & VOLIII-2020

11. Wikipedia on "Brahma Vidya"

12. "Yogapedia on "Brahma Vidya"

13. Tamil book written and published by Dr. Venkatesh MBBs., CCEBDM, MBA. He is a ShishyA of Villur NadAdur, Sri Bhashya SimhAsanam, SAstra SAhitee, Vallaba Vidvanmani, Dr. Sri.

MatuPayave, KarunAkarArya Maha Desikan. The name of the book is Sri Vidyaigalum and Sri. Rajagopalnum (ஸ்ரீவித்யைகளும்ஶ்ரீராஜகோபாலனும்.), மன்னார்குடி ஶ்ரீராஜகோபாலன் செய்தருளியலீலைகளும், அவை உணர்த்தும் உபநிஷத் ப்ரஹ்ம வித்யைகளும். (All LeelAs done by BhagavAn Sri. Mannarkudi Rajagopalan and the way they indicate Upanishad Brahma VidyAs)

14. An introduction to 32 Brahma Vidyas, Secret Doctrines, by Sr. K. R. Krishnaswami., Paduka Krupa, A & K Prakashana, Sep 2011.

15. Srimath Rahasya Traya sAram, Sri Poundarikapuram Swami Asramam, Srirangam published book.-first edition -1960. Proof reading by Sri.U.Ve. VidvAn oppiliappan sannidhi, Vangeepuram Navaneetham Sri.Ramadesikachariar Swami.

16. The Yoga Upanishad's,Sanskrit Text with Commentary of

17. Sri.Upanishad -Brahmayogin-First edition 2019, Jain Amar printing Press-New delhi   (ISBN: 978-81-8315-354-6)

18. Purusha Suktam from श्वेताश्वतरोपनिषद्- Swetasvatara Upanishad -8- https://upanishads.org.in/upanishads/9/3/8

19. https://www.google.co.in/search?q=from+where+this+verse+is+taken+

20. Subhashitani Collections from Net. - https://www.facebook.com/shdve/posts/1360622764454114

21. https://www.tititudorancea.com/z/Bramha vidya_upanishad_sanskrit_devanagari

22. Selections from Minor Upanishads, translated by K. N. Aiyar, 1914 - http://oaks.nvg.org/minor-upanishads.html

23. Bramha Vidya (Chandogya Ch.8) Kindle Edition

24. Ubhaya Vedanta Grantha Mala, Srimad Bhagavad Gita, with Srimad Bhagavad Ramanuja's Bhashya, and Srimad Vedanta Desika's Tatparya Chandrika and Srimad Abhinava Desika Uttamur Viraraghavacharya's detailed Introduction and Rasavada Foot notes. Sri. Uttamur Viraraghavacharya's, centenary Trust, Chennai

25. श्रीव्यासकृत ब्रह्मसूत्राणि, by 44th Pontiff (Azagiya Singer), Sri Ahobila Matam.

26. Nava Ratna Malika, Sri Bhashyam of Sri. Ramanujar with Tamil Transliteration by Sri. U. Ve Tirumalai Caturvedi Shatakrutu Navalpakkam. V. Vasudevachariyar (Vol II, III), Vainavan Kural Publication, Chennai-78, First Publication- Vol II-2017 & VOLIII-2020

27. Wikipedia on "Bramha Vidya"

28. "Yogapedia on "Bramha Vidya"

29. Tamil book written and published by Dr. Venkatesh MBBs., CCEBDM, MBA. He is a ShishyA of Villur NadAdur, Sri Bhashya SimhAsanam, SAstra SAhitee, Vallaba Vidvanmani, Dr. Sri. MatuPayave, KarunAkarArya Maha Desikan. The name of the book is *Sri Vidyaigalum and Sri. Rajagopalnum* (ஸ்ரீவித்யைகளும்ஸ்ரீராஜகோபாலனும்.), மன்னார்குடி ஸ்ரீராஜகோபாலன் செய்தருளியலீலைகளும், அவை உணர்த்தும் உபநிஷத் ப்ரஹ்ம வித்யைகளும். (All LeelAs done by BhagavAn Sri. Mannarkudi Rajagopalan and the way they indicate Upanishad Bramha VidyAs)

30. An introduction to 32 Bramha Vidyas, Secret Doctrines, by Sr. K. R. Krishnaswami., Paduka Krupa, A & K Prakashana, Sep 2011.

31. Srimath Rahasya Traya sAram, Sri Poundarikapuram Swami Asramam, Srirangam published book first edition -1960. Proof reading by Sri.U.Ve. VidvAn oppiliappan sannidhi, Vangeepuram Navaneetham Sri.Ramadesikachariar Swami.

32. The Yoga Upanishad's, Sanskrit Text with Commentary of

33. Sri. Upanishad   -Bramha yogin-First edition 2019, Jai Amar printing Press-New Delhi

34. Srimad Bhagavad Gita (With Srimad Bhagavad Ramanuja's

35. Bhashya and Srimad Vedanta Desika's Tatparya   Chandrika and Srimad Abhinava Desika Uttamur Veerarraghavacharya's. Detailed Introduction and Rasavada Foot Notes. Vedic texts Rig, Sama, Yajur Veda, English Translation by Dr. Tulsi Ram M.A; Ph D(London)

36.   Narayana Guru

37. https://krishnayanam.wordpress.com/2014/05/17/Bramha vidya-panchakam-five-verses-on-the-Bramha n-lore-by-sree-narayana-   guru/

38. Meaning from Chat AI (ब्रह्म सूक्तं-From TB 2.8.8.10,11)